South Africa'S

'BLACK' Market

To Barry,

New colleagues are
the best colleagues,
particularly when they
live next door.

It will be a pleasure
to work with you.

Jeff Falkman

South Africa's

'BLACK' Market

How to Do Business with Africans

Jeffrey A. Fadiman, Ph.D.

INTERCULTURAL PRESS, INC.

For information contact:
Intercultural Press, Inc.
PO Box 700
Yarmouth, ME 04096 USA
207-846-5168
www.interculturalpress.com

Design and production by Patty J. Topel

Printed in the United States of America

04　03　02　01　00　　1　2　3　4　5

Library of Congress Cataloging-in-Publication Data

Fadiman, Jeffrey.
　　South Africa's 'BLACK' Market: how to do business with
Africans / Jeffrey A. Fadiman.
　　　　p.　cm.
　　Includes bibliographical references.
　　ISBN 1-877864-79-X (alk. paper)
　　1. South Africa—Commerce—Handbooks, manuals, etc.
2. South Africa—Economic conditions—1991–　　3. South
Africa—Social conditions—1961–　I. Title.

HF3901.Z6 F335 2000
968—dc21　　　　　　　　　　　　　　　00–038287

Dedication

Katerina Yvonne Hollblad-Fadiman, M.D., M.P.H., C.L.T.
I dedicate this book to you.

Without you, there would be no book. It was you who forced me to begin, twisting my arm until I started to write. Who but you would have shared my lifelong love affair with Africa's animals and thus my joy and wonder, as we walked so many miles that year, along wild paths, among wild beasts, holding hands when we were frightened? Who but you would have patiently endured my love of all things Zulu? Who but you would have listened and listened and listened again to my unending tales of South Africa's past? And who but you would have combed out the tangles in this manuscript, deflecting errors, reweaving ideas, and transforming my prose into pearls?

The Zulu language says it well: *Enhliziyweni yendoda, umkayo uyizimu.* "In the heart of a man, his wife is a giant." *Kunjalo.* It is so. *Ngiyabonga,* Katerina-the-giant, for sharing this book. *Ngiyabonga,* Katerina, for sharing my life. Sharpest critic, closest comrade, precious wife.

—Jeffrey Fadiman
April 2000

Table of Contents

Foreword

I became a friend, supporter, and promoter of South Africa during my first visit there in 1975. Since then my primary work in the international field has been to encourage Western businesses to trade with and invest in the South African economy—easily the most successful economy on the entire African continent as well as the principal hope for the economic recovery of Africa as a whole.

In my twenty-four years of involvement here, I have become increasingly convinced that the Western trading nations must examine the previously unexplored culture of the African peoples. To do this suggests both good business and good sense. If the West is to be of help to Africa, it must come to understand the intricacies of African culture. It must also do so in order to trade and invest in a globally competitive manner.

Indeed, to do business with any foreign people, one must be familiar with their culture. No successful and even faintly competitive financier would present his or her case in the same manner to, say, Indians, Saudi Arabians, Germans, Indonesians, Japanese, or Americans. Their cultures, hugely different, must be meticulously researched in order both to display respect for their perspectives and to predict their responses.

This means that international business investors or managers, considering investment options in South Africa, can no longer leave the study of black African cultures to the anthropologist but must instead walk outside the security and convenience of their offices to personally discover the beliefs, manners, morals, icons, religions, philosophies, laws, and perhaps a hundred other measurements, which together make up a well-entrenched and vibrant culture. In short, they must learn African methods to tap African markets.

This is what Professor Jeffrey A. Fadiman has done. He has combined twenty-eight years of firsthand African field experience with an academic background based on forty publications to learn how Africans do business and thus how we can do business with them. Fadiman does not write in the language of academia. His book is thoroughly researched, but it is aimed at the businessperson who is tightly scheduled, overworked, in demand—and thus must read on the run. You can read *South Africa's 'Black' Market* on the run. It is readable, practical, sometimes controversial, and occasionally frightening. Notwithstanding, his message is simple: "South Africa is, as it has been throughout its history, a new type of wild west: always beautiful, often dangerous, only for the bold."

—Dr. Anthony G. Cadman
Chairman, Anthony Cadman Associates
London and Durban, 2000

Acknowledgments

One real joy in writing a book is thanking those who made it a pleasure. It becomes even better when I include those individuals who do not yet know I exist. Thus, my thanks go out to:

Dr. Anthony G. Cadman, Chairman of Anthony Cadman Associates, consultants to South African and British firms about investment in South Africa. Thank you for sharing twenty-four years of on-site corporate and personal experience. You have taught me more about South Africa's Africans than I could ever have hoped to learn.

Marshall Burak, Dean of the College of Business, San Jose State University, for greater financial and personal support than I had any right to hope for.

Linda Rhoad, South Africa branch of the Fulbright Scholarship Program, for guiding me across the maze of predeparture land mines.

Robin Morris, author of *Marketing to Black Townships: Practical Guidelines,* for convincing me that township marketing could actually be done. Your work inspired mine.

Mary de Haas, lecturer, social anthropology, University of Natal, for your research on political violence in Natal. Your courage in researching the politically incorrect gave me the courage to do the same.

David Varty and Alan Berstein, cofounders of the Conservation Corporation of Africa, for pioneering the concept of "relationship marketing" in the field of ecotourism that this book recommends. Your thinking has inspired mine.

Dirk Rezelman, Chief of Public Affairs at the University of Zululand; and Paul Denig, United States Information Service, for guiding me into the turbulent surf of the University of Zululand (Unizul), then keeping me afloat when the waves grew high.

Volker Hooyberg, Marieke Burger, Tony Kruger, Robert Ntuli, and Petro Mersham, for teaching me how to swim in that turbulence and pulling me off the rocks each time I foundered.

Gary Mersham, for first suggesting that I try the waters, then writing the letters to key people that made it a reality.

The 364 Unizul communications students who overflowed my classes, sitting on steps, floors, and windowsills, and staying awake when the heat reached 44 degrees centigrade inside the classrooms. Thank you for patiently correcting my Zulu language missteps and teaching me far more than I taught you.

Toby Frank, president of Intercultural Press; David Hoopes, editor in chief; and Judy Carl-Hendrick, managing editor, for transforming a conventional business relationship into a long-term friendship and transforming me from an unknown author into one of the IPI family.

Ngiyabongeni, bantu bonke. Thank you, one and all.

Introduction: South Africa's 'Black' Market

> South Africa is the most exotic place I can
> imagine, the one I most want to visit, and the last
> with which my firm could consider doing
> business.
> —U.S. entrepreneur

African Businesswoman

This book, like many, first sprang from a dream—but not my dream. It was the dream of a tall, statuesque, and unusually daring African businesswoman. In today's apartheid-free South Africa, many African women now dream of launching a business. Some are drawn to American business methods and thus apply for grants or training. This woman dreamed a different kind of dream; she wanted to market African business methods to Americans—not easy in a country where most of us do not realize that such methods even exist. Raised in Southern Africa, she was educated to become a secretary. Learning those skills, she taught them to others, at first just in her own office. Later, she launched a firm, training women to work in other offices. At first she followed Western models, using U.S. business texts. Then, she modified her training methods to match African business needs.

Her dream expanded accidentally. Her little firm was noticed by a much larger U.S. company that specialized in office training. It sent a representative to buy her out in order to acquire her physical plant and clientele. Instead, they offered her a franchise, through which she would transmit their office training methods to her client base. On impulse, she refused. Instead, *she* offered to franchise her African office training methods to Americans, using the representative's firm as *her* base. The American laughed pleasantly and instantly dismissed the concept, not even inquiring which methods she had in mind.

Offended, she decided—again on impulse—to fly to the United States and formally present her concept to the firm's CEO. Her husband opposed the idea, arguing that her finances, education, and English were too limited. Nor had she any U.S. contacts. Doggedly, she developed them, to the point where one eventually helped her reach me. Her proposal was direct: Would I teach her how Americans do business and thus help her market an African concept in ways American executives would understand?

The training interested us both, but although her English steadily improved, we failed to communicate. I had researched African marketing methods; she had studied Western books. Nonetheless, we based our business strategies on different logic. What I saw as useful in American terms struck her as alien. Nor did I think her African sales techniques would impress U.S. executives. Nonetheless, we blended our ideas to create a strategy we both felt might work.

It failed. The firm's officers listened politely, then rejected her concept without query or comment, just as their field representative had done earlier. They were simply uninterested, she said later, in African business methods. Instead they asked her once again if she would franchise their methods in her region. That was, she felt, their actual purpose in agreeing to meet with her. She had flown eight thousand miles simply to hear them ignore her offer and repeat theirs. She left for Africa in anger, and her last comment stung: "They listen but don't hear. How can they do business in South Africa without learning how South Africans do business? You are a writer. Write a book to tell them what we do." Then she was gone.

American Businessman

Weeks later an American business contact called me. He had been assigned to start a venture in South Africa, was to leave in thirty days, and was quite worried. He knew a good deal about his product but nothing of its intended market. His firm was small, its start-up capital limited, and this was his first time overseas as a project manager. He wanted to prepare but did not know how; nor did senior members of his firm. Curious, I telephoned them to ask how they meant to prepare him. They replied that no formal training was required for any overseas assignment. Instead, they chose the man (always a man) they felt might best adjust. That meant sending single males with high U.S. performance ratings in the belief that top domestic performers with no home ties would always find their foreign footing.

My caller's company is thoroughly mainstream. Few U.S. firms train the managers they send abroad in foreign business methods (Rhinesmith 1991). Less than half provide foreign area training (Runzheimer 1996). One company sent a friend of mine to Bahrain. They gave her one training brochure, which declared that the country was Muslim, Friday was holy, the climate was hot, the beaches were splendid, and little else. One male contact, placed in Saudi Arabia to launch a U.S. supermarket, was arrested hours after his store opened for playing background music during the public call to prayer. This type of conflict was precisely what my caller hoped to avoid. He wanted to obey local law, adhere to custom, and do business in local ways. However, knowing nothing about them, he did not know what to learn.

He is not alone. Africa is our commercial blind spot. We have ignored it since the 1960s and know nothing of its business methods. Glance at books in any bookstore that deal with doing business overseas. Many address Europe, Asia, Eastern Europe, South America, and the Middle East. None are directed toward Africa, let alone using African methods to do business there. As a business destination, Africa has vanished from American itineraries.

In consequence, South Africa's Africans have vanished as well, at least from our commercial agendas. During the apartheid era, corporate strategists perceived them as politically oppressed, economically exploited, and devoid of buying power. The 1994 political shift from white to black rule (known in South Africa as "The Turn") briefly captured American commercial attention. Nonetheless, most U.S. firms focused on the wealthy white population, ignoring its "poorer" black population.

However, many of South Africa's Africans are not poor. They form the largest black upper, middle, and working classes on the continent. Yet, few Americans recognize their economic potential and fewer use African methods to tap it. Notwithstanding, these methods have been honed and polished by distinguished African mercantile clans, who have formed notable, sophisticated, and successful trading companies across the continent for the past one thousand years. Surely they have much to teach us.

My caller believed I had much to teach him. We worked together until he went overseas. However, as had been the case with my African female colleague, we initially failed to communicate. I knew African methods; he had read U.S. business books. He knew what worked in America; I knew what would not work in South Africa. Despite these differences, however, we developed a workable strategy before he finally flew off to Johannesburg. His farewell, however, echoed hers: "Good ideas. Write a book."

Why Me?

Bad advice? Surely, books on marketing to Africans should be written by Africans, not Americans. Admittedly, I had spent time in Africa. When I was twenty, I paddled a canoe up West Africa's Niger River to the city of Timbuktu. Thereafter, I taught in East African schools, where my students force-fed me Swahili. I then became a safari guide, teaching Americans how to live with and love Africa's wildlife. None of that, of course, qualified me to write this book. Both adventuring and teaching kept me safely on the Western side of an invisible wall that divides African lifestyles from those of foreign guests. What I did, I did in Western fashion, thus remaining very much a stranger in that foreign land.

On my next try, however, I did pass through that wall. Seeking a Ph.D. in tropical history, I won a Fulbright Scholarship to record the oral history of a then-isolated Kenyan tribe. To do that, I had to locate its oldest living men, then in their eighties and scattered across the rain forest slopes of Mt. Kenya.

I found them. Over one hundred fragile elders taught me their ancestral traditions and with them a coherent and logical system of thought. We might label it a tribal philosophy; they called it "elders' wisdom." I spent eighteen months at their evening fires, listening, tape-recording, and trying to grasp not merely what they said but how they thought. Now, with thirty years of hindsight, I see why they called it "wisdom." They had explained not only how they had behaved historically but also the logic guiding that behavior; not merely what they did (and do) but why as well. In short, these one hundred teachers taught me a different way to deal with life.

Years later, again returning to Africa as a Fulbright scholar, I found the same system of thought, this time among South Africa's Africans. They share the traditions of those elders from Kenya, as do Africans across the continent. With allowance for regional variations, this means most Africans still hold cultural, religious, legal, and commercial philosophies in common. In short, they often think along similar lines, solving problems in similar ways.

In business, for instance, most Africans practice what American business now calls "relationship marketing," a system in which creating relationships with one another supplements and often takes precedence over the drive to maximize financial profit. Although speaking different languages, most Africans share a common past and thus a common culture, including business culture.

Reflecting on this similarity, I then explored those aspects of this common business culture that foreigners might find useful in today's commercial scene. This book, therefore, is written for anyone—in business, development, diplomacy, health, tourism, et cetera—who wishes to learn more about Africans in order to work more closely with them, anywhere. From this point on, however, I will use the word *Africans* to refer to the indigenous peoples of South Africa—and thus avoid unending repetition of the phrase "South African Africans." Only when context demands will I use the same word to refer to those who live in other African regions or the continent as a whole, and those instances will be clearly distinguished.

Why You?

I have written this material for Americans of every color. Most observers share my opinion that African Americans who seek business opportunities in South Africa do about as well as Euro-Americans, Asian Americans, and so on. They also suffer similar criticisms. Black and white Americans alike have been described, by South Africans of every color, as nonracist, flexible, friendly, enthusiastic, and eager to learn. They are simultaneously perceived as patronizing, arrogant, unwilling to learn African languages, contemptuous of local tradition, and hesitant to socialize with Africans (Daley 1998). In sum, South Africans perceive us all as belonging to one tribe—which is how we should perceive ourselves.

This book is also meant for Americans of both sexes. It is unfortunate that our language often uses *he* or *businessman* in situations that obviously apply to both men and women. Nonetheless, any writer who, for the sake of political correctness, is willing to fill an entire book with the terms *he/she, business man/-woman*, and so forth risks wearying readers before they reach page thirty.

In fact, U.S. businesswomen do not suffer visible discrimination in most African commercial circles. They meet, eat, drink, negotiate, and make decisions as do men. Consequently, (though regretfully) I will use the terms *he* and *businessman* when describing situations where I feel both sexes face similar commercial problems and where the use of plural forms makes awkward reading.

The ideas in this book are often politically incorrect. They often violate the Golden Rule of American Africanists: Thou shalt speak no evil of Africans. Only one writer, to my knowledge, has confronted the taboo with courage:

> Maybe I should have just written a standard book
> on Africa that would have talked broadly about
> the politics, the possibilities, the prospects for
> change. But I'm tired of lying. And I'm tired of
> all the ignorance and hypocrisy and the double
> standards I hear and read about Africa, much of
> it from people who have never been there....
> (Richburg 1997, xii)

Maybe I, too, should have just written a standard book, one that talks broadly and glowingly about the country's future prospects while unstintingly praising the reign of Nelson Mandela. However, the tale I have to tell deals with employing African methods to succeed in South Africa's African markets. To do that, I must discuss the undiscussable—South Africa's current level of crime, which is third worst in the world, as well as the impact on U.S. firms of that government's failure to cope.

Many South Africans (and Americans) object to my doing this. One Capetonian, after reading parts of my text, argued hotly that if I "actually write that these frightful things are happening, no American enterprises will come." Unfortunately, these frightful things are happening. Fortunately, American enterprises still come, and it is better that they arrive forewarned. To deliberately ignore African problems does the African people no favor. Conversely, to expose, publicize, and even criticize them can provide a chance to change. In consequence, my writing will be as politically incorrect as South African circumstances warrant.

Finally, this book is written for the commercial pioneer, the risk taker, the path breaker. In a military setting, he would be called the point man. The point man is first in his unit to penetrate unknown and possibly unfriendly areas. He risks a hostile response. In business, he is the first in his unit to deal with local people, contend with local custom, and confront local law. He too risks a hostile response. He may work quite alone or represent a small firm, with start-up funds so limited that it cannot afford to waste a dollar in miscalculations and mistakes. Nor do the heads of such firms invariably possess extensive global expertise. Indeed, their managers may know nothing of South Africa; that is why they send a point man: to pioneer.

This book is meant for pioneers. It will cut a whole new path through South Africa's commercial jungles. In recommending that you read it, I assume you plan to move beyond South Africa's smaller (and shrinking) "White market" of some nine million Europeans and into the huge (and expanding) "Black market" of perhaps forty million Africans—and then toward the estimated four hundred million other African consumers beyond South Africa's borders. If so, why not use African marketing methods to enter their markets?

Chapter 1 begins the day you first decide to launch a South African venture. I shall assume you are still in the United States. I assume further that your knowledge of American business is thorough, that your experience in South Africa is limited, and that you plan to research its postapartheid lifestyle. That may be harder than it seems, for the land is in constant transition; some would say constant turmoil. Its business environment is thus less predictable and carries greater risk than ours.

I will therefore explore the most commercially difficult, professionally irritating, and privately frightening racial, tribal, commercial, managerial, ecological, social, and criminal problems you will face in launching a first-time venture. I will also suggest pragmatic, on-site options (often, African options) to help resolve them. Where possible, I will draw these approaches directly from South Africa's commercial scene. Where relevant, I will present other alternatives that have worked elsewhere (in Africa, Asia, the United States, etc.) and that may prove effective in South Africa as well. Thus, in one sense, this book is a beginners' guide; in another, it is a survival guide. In every sense, it is a marketing guide, designed to provide an intricate and in-depth introduction to South Africa's 'Black' market.

References

Daley, Suzanne. 1998. "For Black Americans in Black South Africa—A Chilly Reception." *San Francisco Chronicle* (8 April), 2.

Rhinesmith, Stephen. 1991. "An Agenda for Globalization." *Training and Development Journal* (February).

Richburg, Keith. 1997. *Out of Africa.* New York: Basic Books, HarperCollins.

Runzheimer International Newsletter. 1996. Cited in *New York Times* (15 September).

1

Start-Up Venture: Start-Up Questions

South Africa is unique. It is the one African country where it is possible to work in the third world, reside and relax in the first world and remain permanently in the dark.

—British businessman

Lay of the Land: Where Are the Markets?

South Africa is vast. Where are the most attractive markets? Look at a map from south to north. Begin at the Cape of Good Hope. Usually marketers glance at the city of Cape Town, then notice the coastal zone surrounding it, a narrow band with fertile soil and temperate climate. Usually referred to as "the Cape," it produces a traditional range of Mediterranean crops, including fruit, grain, and superb wines.

Behind the coastal zone the land climbs in three huge steps to form low, middle, and high plateaus—known respectively as the Little, Great, and Upper Karroo. *Karroo* means "thirstland." The Little Karroo gets less rain than the Cape and is thus less fertile. The Great Karroo is still more arid, while the Upper Karroo is driest of all. Inland, this last plateau merges into the High Veld, a vast and originally treeless grassland. As you move north and west across this veld, the aridity intensifies until it merges in turn into the Kalahari Desert. For marketers, this means the narrow southern coast can support dense populations, while the higher, drier inland zones cannot.

Now look at the map from east to west. Winds blow west off the Indian Ocean, over another narrow band of fertile coastline, then reach an ascending set of irregular terraces similar to the three Karroos. These lead up through the Low Veld and then the Middle Veld (or Bushveld) regions (similar to the two lower Karroos) and once more up to the High Veld. There, the wind sweeps west across flat, increasingly arid land until it reaches the Kalahari Desert.

However, one part of the High Veld continues to climb. It is partially surrounded by a mountain range that forms a quarter circle twelve hundred miles long. The highest peaks, the

Map 1

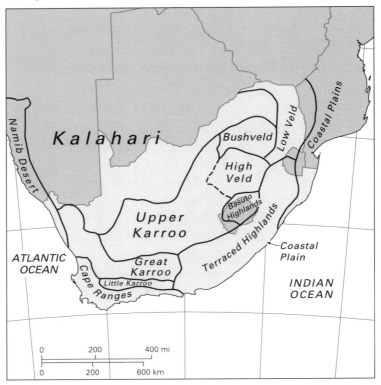

Drakensberg (Dragon Mountains), reach twelve thousand feet to form steep, flat-topped mesas. Part of this mountain wall is fairly near South Africa's wet East Coast. This means it blocks the inland flow of rains, drenching the fertile coastline but leaving higher regions dry. In consequence, as in the Cape, these narrow, wet east coastal zones can support many people, while the vast, dry inland regions cannot (Fitzgerald 1961).

Historically, it has been the fertile, rain-drenched East Coast Corridor that has attracted huge numbers of African migrants over the past ten centuries. Far smaller numbers settled the desert, veld, and mountains. Similarly, the fertile, moist Cape drew European migrants after 1600, but almost no one moved inland. Today's demographics still partially reflect those early migrations. The narrow coasts support dense populations while the arid interior does not. In consequence, the most demographically attractive markets (outside of cities) run north to south along the eastern coast to the Cape, whereas the least attractive (again, excluding cities) are in the interior: mountains, desert, and veld.

South Africa has recently been divided into nine provinces. The former Cape Province was split into Western, Eastern, and Northern Cape. The old Transvaal became Northern Province, Northwest Province, and Mpumalanga. The urbanized Johannesburg/Pretoria zone is now Gauteng. Natal was renamed KwaZulu-Natal, while the Orange Free State became Free State Province but retained its original boundaries. From a commercial perspective, the largest number of potential clientele live (in descending order) within Gauteng, KwaZulu-Natal, Western Cape, and Eastern Cape. The others have far fewer people, thus much smaller markets.

These provinces are linked by an impressive infrastructure. Tarred roads cross the country. Trains and long-distance buses operate on time. Short-haul bus lines plod irregularly across rural areas, while minivans serve the cities. Cellular telephones provide intermittent service along main highways. The price of one cellular unit has dropped from $700 to $208 in

Map 2

supermarkets and to $83 in black markets, with two million subscribers expected in the near future. The Ga-Seleka telecenter now provides e-mail, fax, and Internet services to four hundred thousand people within fifty miles in all directions from Johannesburg. Five TV channels and nine types of radio stations blanket urban and rural regions. One international and several domestic airlines provide on-time service. South Africa also uses wind and solar energy, as 250,000 windmills now dot the coasts, and solar cells tap sunshine over three hundred days per year.

The land has one more advantage; it is a scenic paradise. The rolling hills of the East Coast Corridor virtually glow with mile on mile of green and glistening sugarcane. Higher up, the hills are covered with waving "sweetgrass" that calls out to be walked through. As one climbs inland, the land evolves into miles of clifflike mesas, which gradually transform themselves once more into the massive and majestic Drakensberg.

Flowers, birds, and animals are far more visible than in the United States. South Africa has 5,000 kinds of flowers, 870 bird species, 43 marine categories, and 290 varieties of mammal (Motavelli 1995). That means that 7 percent of the world's creatures live in this 1 percent of its land mass. As a result most cities, towns, and many villages have their own tiny wildlife reserves, complete with monkeys, birds, and plains game. I lived in such a village in Zululand and could pass by monkeys, zebra, antelope, and fish eagles while walking my dog. There are also seventeen national wildlife parks. Plans exist to merge no fewer than seven of these into one massive biosphere that will create the largest wilderness on earth. Surely, South Africa can be a pleasant place to do business.

Where Are the Urban Markets?

South Africa's older maps can be deceptive. Some still depict the country as having three large cities (Cape Town, Durban, Johannesburg) and six small ones (Pretoria, Kimberley, Port Elizabeth, East London, Pietermaritzburg, Bloemfontein). All other urban zones are classified as towns or villages, which during apartheid were reserved for Whites. However, marketers will find this description inaccurate. In fact, each former white municipality (large or small) is surrounded by one, two, or several African urban areas, all far larger than the white zone in their center.

Under apartheid, these were called native reserves or locations. After military defeat by Whites, the tribes were moved to rural locations—as Americans enclosed each defeated Indian nation in separate Indian reservations. Urban locations emerged later. These were basically male labor compounds, whose thousands of workers were bussed daily into white urban areas to work, then transported back at dusk to eat and sleep. These locations were not considered towns or cities. Thus, few older maps included them. Other maps showed the reserves but not their size, perhaps because no mapmaker could learn how many people lived in each. No African could legally live outside a location; no White could live in one. Today, these areas are called townships.

Since The Turn, of course, any South African citizen may live anywhere. In demographic terms, this means each former white municipality, whether a village, town, or city, has begun to blend with its surrounding African locations to form much differently configured urban units. Johannesburg, for instance, has become an African city. Each morning fleets of minivans deliver thousands of sellers, shoppers, and job hunters from Soweto (South West Township) and every other nearby township into the formerly white business district

> where Zairian hawkers peddle...Mozambican barbers shear locks...and at the fast-food Africa hut...shoppers fortify themselves with ox tail soup and pap (cornmeal mush). There are few white faces, but Africans are too busy making and spending money to fret. (Mabry 1996, 47)

However, even this picture is distorted, for it still depicts Soweto and the other townships as adjacent bedroom suburbs rather than emerging cities. Urban Soweto hums with entrepreneurial activity. For decades, it was depicted by the U.S. media as a center of oppression, racial riots, police brutality, and grinding poverty. Today it holds an estimated four million people. The average household contains 5.2 individuals, who earn $555 per capita annual income. Most homes have sewerage, electricity, and running water (Menaker 1995). Incomes in the wealthy section are said to equal those in the United States.

More important, Soweto is developing a commercial core. Its first shopping mall mixes national retail chains with African-owned cinemas, food outlets, banks, beauty salons, and supermarkets; a hotel and casino have also been proposed. Other townships have similar intentions. Indeed, the whole Gauteng region is expected to become South Africa's first industrial megacity—a development no U.S. manager should ignore.

South Africa's other cities display similar demographic changes. Durban's central city is almost wholly African. Whites and Indians live in adjacent suburbs, while most Blacks reside in surrounding townships. However, thousands of Africans have seized land adjacent to both white and Indian homes, creating massive squatter settlements. Cape Town's urban core is multiracial. Whites live in suburbs, while most nonwhites live in nearby townships and commute to the city, either to seek work or to perform it. The six smaller cities follow a similar pattern. Each day, they swell in size, as hundreds (or thousands) of Africans enter former white areas to work, shop, visit, and then depart at dusk for home locations. The same applies, on a smaller scale, to every town. Urban markets are thus far larger than they seem, since they now include the thousands upon thousands of township clientele. See map 2.

Segment the Markets: Who Lives Where?

Indigenous Africans

One way to subdivide this massive market is to learn where each ethnic group lives as well as the terms used throughout South Africa to identify it. Thus, the words *Black, Bantu,* and *African* all denote South Africans of ethnic African (negroid) heritage, whose ancestors entered the area some four hundred to one thousand years ago.

About 41–43 million Blacks (estimates vary widely) make up approximately 76 percent of the population. They are also known as *Bantu,* a word derived from the term *AbaNtu,* which means "people" in ten of South Africa's African languages. The Bantu extend across South, East, and Central Africa in a huge ethnic rectangle that extends from South Africa's tip north to central Kenya and west to the coasts of today's Congo and Cameroon.

Two thousand years ago their ancestors spoke a common language that scholars have labeled "original Bantu." This subsequently fragmented into hundreds of the current Bantu languages and thousands of dialects. Nonetheless, all of the languages use the word *AbaNtu* to mean "people." They also share common grammar and vocabulary. Thus, it is linguistically correct to say that all South Africa's Bantu people speak one of the related Bantu languages.

Within South Africa, Bantu speakers form three language groups. Over time, the two largest groups subdivided into tribes, each speaking a contemporary Bantu language. The largest is the *Nguni* group (over seventeen million): Swazi, Shangaan/Tsonga, Zulu, Xhosa, and Ndebele. Their ancestors migrated into the East Coast Corridor. Four of the five Nguni-speaking peoples now live primarily along the corridor, spilling over into those High Veld regions closest to it. Large numbers also work in Durban, Johannesburg, Port Elizabeth, East London, and (more recently) Cape Town.

From north to south along the corridor, the Nguni divide as follows:

Figure 1

Nguni Language Group	Population	Principal Location
Swazi	1 million	N. KwaZulu-Natal
Shangaan/Tsonga	750,000	N.E. KwaZulu-Natal
Zulu	8–9 million	KwaZulu-Natal
Xhosa	6–7 million	E. Cape Province
Ndebele	670,000	High Veld

All Nguni speakers can communicate with one another and share a common culture.

The second largest language group (eight million) is called *Sotho* (pronounced "Sutu"). Their ancestors entered today's South Africa to the east of coastal Nguni and migrated southward onto the High Veld. They now include Tswana (once known as West Sotho), Northern Sotho, and Southern Sotho.

Figure 2

Sotho Language Group	Population	Principal Location
Tswana	3 million	Northwest Province
Northern Sotho	4 million	Gauteng, Mpumalanga, Northern Province
Southern Sotho	1 million	Free State, Republic of Lesotho

All Sotho speakers can communicate with one another (but not with the Nguni) and share a common culture.

South Africa's smallest Bantu group is the *Venda* (500,000–600,000), who live in Northern Province, near Zimbabwe. They communicate with outside groups by learning other languages.

A fourth African group is more difficult to classify. Since 1994 between two and eight million foreign Africans (estimates vary), born outside South Africa, have entered the country illegally. Most are from the Southern African nations of Mozambique, Zimbabwe, Lesotho, Namibia, and Swaziland. Some come from every nation in East and Central Africa, which means they too share elements of the Bantu language and lifestyle. Others come from West Africa and speak other tongues. They cluster in the urban squatter fringes. Although poor, they may emerge as significant market segments once established.

Two smaller groups should also be mentioned, the *Khoi* and the *San,* often referred to collectively as *KhoiSan.* They are South Africa's earliest inhabitants, having occupied the area thousands of years before either Bantu or Dutch migrants intruded from the north and south. They form a distinct ethnic unit, with physical, cultural, and linguistic characteristics that are neither black nor white. Neither group refers to itself as KhoiSan. The San, who speak four unrelated languages, refer to one another by clan names. Until recently, Europeans called them *bushmen,* a label now considered insulting. Avoid it. Many

San now work as scouts, either in game parks or for the army.

The Khoi (or *KhoiKhoi*) originally called themselves *Khoikhoin* (men of men). Early Cape Dutch renamed them *Hottentots* (stammerers, stutterers). The term came from the seventeenth-century Dutch phrase *hatern en tatern* (stammer and stutter) and reflected a Dutch perception of the many tongue clicks in KhoiSan languages (Tanzer 1997). Today, *Hottentot* is considered offensive, as is the abbreviated *hotnot*. Few Khoi remain in South Africa. Most live in adjoining Namibia, where they refer to themselves as the "red nations," to differentiate themselves from "black nations" to their north.

You will also want to learn which words (some now corrupted) have acquired "racialist" (racist) connotations. The word *tribe*, for example, is perceived as racist by some American academics, who feel it depicts a primitive social structure and thus instantly labels the Africans (and the speakers) as primitive. Most Africans disagree, using the term to reflect descent from a single ancestor with a common kinship, culture, history, tradition, and language. Avoid it in U.S. academic circles, but since Africans use it freely in South Africa, so can you.

Two other words, however, do have racist connotations. The word *Munt* (from MuNtu, which means "person" in all Bantu languages) is a racist insult. Similarly, the word *Kaffir,* originally an Arabic term meaning "black, pagan, and non-Muslim," was borrowed by Whites as a racial insult when referring to Africans. It is now as offensive as the word *nigger* is in America. Do not use either.

Immigrant Africans

The terms *White, European,* and *Westerner* refer to South Africans of European heritage, even though their ancestors may have lived in South Africa (or another African nation) for up to four hundred years. These terms also include white (but not black) Americans, Canadians, Australians, and so on. In 1996 Whites numbered some 9.3 million, or an estimated 11 to 13.6

percent of the population. They form two major language groups and six minor ones. Sixty percent are *Afrikaner,* who form 7 percent of the population (Daley 1998). They are descended from Cape Dutch migrants who later trekked into the African interior and renamed themselves to indicate they were no longer Dutch but African.

Afrikaners who subsequently settled in Transvaal and the Orange Free State also refer to themselves as *Boers* (farmers), a term that once identified all Dutch South Africans. Those who first migrated from the Cape into these two regions were known historically as *trekboers* (walking cattle farmers) and/ or *voortrekkers* (advance migrants, i.e., pioneers). Today, all three terms may carry racial connotations, since many Africans now use them to label Whites they consider racist.

Just under 40 percent of the remaining Whites call themselves *British,* thus suggesting they originated either from the United Kingdom or one of its former African colonies. They form just under 5 percent of the population. Other Europeans come from Portugal (via Angola or Mozambique), Belgium (via Rwanda, Burundi, or Congo), Germany (via Cameroon or Namibia), Lithuania, Russia, and Greece. There are virtually no South African Americans.

Europeans live in the cities and towns. Fewer than six thousand actually farm, but most who do are Afrikaners. Until The Turn, Afrikaners also comprised most of the civil service, courts, police, and army. An estimated three million live in the Free State, Gauteng, and the former Transvaal. Some two million British South Africans live primarily along the coasts in Western and Eastern Cape and KwaZulu-Natal. Highly urbanized, they provide most of the banking, commercial, and professional personnel.

The term *Coloured (the Coloured, Coloureds)* refers to a now distinct ethnic group that emerged from sexual unions between Whites, Blacks, Malay-Indonesians, and KhoiSan, the region's earliest inhabitants. Most Coloureds have adopted Afrikaner religion, culture, language, lifestyle, and economic aspirations. Note that the spelling differs from the American *colored*. Note also that the phrase "the Coloured" lacks the negative connotation it would have in the United States. Some four million Coloureds live in or near Cape Town and Western Cape Province. Many fish, farm, or herd; others work for Whites. Many others have entered business, teaching, and the professions. They make up an estimated 8.6 to 9 percent of the population.

The word *Asian* refers primarily to Indians but also to immigrants from Pakistan, Fiji, China, and often Cape Malay. In fact the original Cape Malays were Javanese and Sumatrans, part of today's Indonesia. Most were nobles and warriors, defeated by the invading Dutch in the 1600s and sent to the Cape

Map 3

as slaves. Since Malays and Indonesians speak variants of the same language, they were mislabeled on landing and became known as Cape Malays. Some integrated into the Coloureds. Others have existed as a separate Cape community for four hundred years, retaining many Malay-Indonesian traditions as well as the Islamic faith.

The Indians were originally brought from British India in the 1860s to grow sugar in Natal. An estimated one million of their descendants live in or near Durban, with smaller populations in other urban areas. They make up perhaps 3 percent of the population. None work the land; most are in business or the professions.

Should You Market in a Local Language?

You may decide to reach potential clientele through one of the major regional languages as well as in one of the urban dialects. The Zulu language has a written literature, is taught in universities, and is used in both electronic and print media. Nonetheless, it is not a national language but a regional one. It is universal in Durban and across Kwazulu-Natal and can be used to reach speakers of Swazi, Shangaan/Tsonga, and Ndebele, both in their respective homelands and in Gauteng. The Xhosa language is also regional. It is taught in some universities and appears in the media across Eastern Cape and is also used in Cape Town and Gauteng. The same applies to Sotho/Tswana, which can be used in Johannesburg, within Gauteng, and across the Northwest, Northern, and Mpumalanga Provinces. The Venda language is restricted to their homeland.

The Afrikaans language is less regional. Having evolved from seventeenth-century Cape Dutch, it is spoken by Afrikaners throughout the country as well as the Coloureds of Cape. It is the primary language for some 15 percent of the population. Afrikaans has an extensive written literature, is taught in every university, and is used in all media—but it has commercial limitations. Until The Turn all British South Africans learned it in school. In consequence, most read and speak it fluently though they often refuse to do so, preferring to patronize both print and electronic media that utilize English.

African consumers often display a similar response. Under apartheid, African children were forced to study in Afrikaans rather than English. Many therefore still perceive it as a language of oppression and will not use it. Nor will they respond to marketing appeals that do. The language can be used most effectively in Western Cape, Northern Cape, Free State, Johannesburg, and Gauteng.

English is the language of business and the cities. It is taught in all schools and universities; it is also used in the media. Consequently, most Afrikaners speak it fluently, as do all Asians and many urban Coloureds and Bantu. Americans must realize, however, that many business contacts will speak English better than they read and write it, and they may feel uneasy even when speaking. They may prefer to do business in their own language. *English is not universal.* In fact, it predominates only near cities. The rural communities that ring these urban centers, even in once-English colonies, now tend toward Bantu languages or Afrikaans.

Three of the emerging urban dialects may also prove of commercial value. *Towni Sotho* is a distinct urban dialect in Johannesburg that is particularly attractive to Sotho youth, who claim it as their own. *Fanagalo* (Do it like this) is an adult urban pidgin that has become a language of working-class Gauteng. It has been used for 130 years and blends Bantu grammar with Zulu, Xhosa, English, and Afrikaner words. As Blacks came from across South Africa to work in the mines of Johannesburg, they needed to speak to Whites and with one another. As a result, they developed this unique and vibrant pidgin. From the mines, Fanagalo spread to other industries as well as to Bantu domestic servants, who used it to speak with white housewives. It is now so widely used in Gauteng that teaching texts have appeared.

Or consider the commercial potential of *Tsotsi Taal* (gangster slang). Originally developed by gangsters in townships near Johannesburg, Tsotsi Taal evolved from scattered slang into a dialect now widely understood among Gauteng's working and squatter populations, especially among the young, who consider it "cool." It is solely a spoken dialect, but if used artfully, it may attract a youthful urban clientele.

Each of these languages is regional. The one you select for further study will depend on where you launch a venture. If you are based in Cape Town, I would suggest learning Xhosa (over Afrikaans), since 250,000 Xhosa-speakers have come there since 1994 and hundreds of thousands will follow. In Northern Cape, I would use Afrikaans. In Eastern Cape, learn Xhosa. If you are based in Durban and KwaZulu, study Zulu. In Northern, Northwest, and Mpumalanga Provinces, as well as Free State, try Sotho (over Tswana). If you are based in Johannesburg or Gauteng, where no language dominates, I would consider Fanagalo.

A South African language can become your single most valuable business tool. Even your first attempts will please those who hear you. Subsequent study may help to create genuine bonds, while achieving fluency may bind you to South African friends for life. In the words of former President Nelson Mandela: "Without language, one cannot talk to people.... One cannot share their aspirations, grasp their history, appreciate their poetry or savour their songs" (1994, 97).

There are also practical reasons to begin learning an African language. One is to avoid becoming stereotyped by the Africans you meet. Their history is marked by centuries of White conquest. Depending on the victor, defeated Africans were forced to learn either Afrikaans or English, while victorious Europeans derided their Bantu languages as primitive. As a result, few Blacks now expect any White to use their language. They certainly do not expect it of white Americans—or any Americans. We are famous for thinking we need not learn foreign languages.

These adverse expectations are the first reason why you should start learning at least one black South African language. You will do more than shatter their stereotypes. Your struggles with an African language convey respect for African culture. In South Africa, where that culture has been scorned for centuries, your efforts may trigger respect, empathy, and a foundation for future business interaction. When I began to study Zulu, I once greeted an elder with due formality as he passed. Surprised, he asked me why I spoke his language. Surprised in turn, I stammered that I hoped to make friends. "You have," he replied, and we are friends today.

This need to make friends provides a second reason to begin language studies. In the United States we market goods and services. If those prove trustworthy, our business ventures thrive. Among Africans, we must first market ourselves. Only if we seem trustworthy will they consider our goods and services.

Yet trust is hard to build in nations scarred by ethnic conflict. The Blacks I meet have known years of oppression by Whites. Often, as they walk toward me, their expressions chill as they see my color. Only when I greet them in their language do their faces dissolve into those shining smiles that mark the start of African relationships. Only then do talk and laughter begin to create the empathy that is prerequisite to building trust. This expectation is the same in commercial settings. Only after you establish personal ties will they consider your business, and to achieve these ties, you need to learn a Bantu language. It will prove more effective than describing your product.

One final reason to learn a Bantu language is to penetrate the logic of South African culture. To learn how they speak is to grasp how they think. African logic differs from ours. It can follow paths we find tangential and indirect, with which we grow impatient and intolerant. Rather than examining that logic, we denounce it as primitive. Nonetheless, to study a language means learning the logic of its speakers and exploring twists and turns in their words and their minds. What better way to research client needs than to learn the ways in which they talk about them.

References

Daley, Suzanne. 1998. "Dark Past, Black Future for Africa's 'White Tribe'." *New York Times* (27 February), 1, 9.

Fitzgerald, Walter. 1961. *Africa: A Social, Political and Economic Geography of Its Major Regions*. London: Methuen, 148–52.

Mabry, Marcus. 1996. "Johannesburg: Ever Continental." *Newsweek* (10 June), 47.

Mandela, Nelson. 1994. *Long Walk to Freedom*. London: Abacus Books, Little, Brown.

Menaker, Drusilla. 1995. "Soweto, South Africa: Brisk Business in the Townships." *Business Week* (25 September), 126.

Motavelli, Jim. 1995. "Africa Awakes: Ecotourism Offers High Hopes to a South Africa Finally Free of Apartheid." *E Magazine* (March/April), 40.

Tanzer, Jordy. 1997. "Crossroads: All Over the Maps." *Escape* (Winter), 18.

2

Tribalism and Racism: Still Marketing Risks

Wit man moet altyd baas wees; Kaffer op sy
plek. (White man must always be boss; Nigger in
his place.)
　　　　　　—South African election slogan, 1948

It was a crime to walk through a Whites Only
door, a crime to ride a Whites Only bus…a crime
to be unemployed and a crime to be employed in
the wrong place, a crime to live in certain places
and a crime to have no place to live.
　　　　　　　　　　　　　—Nelson Mandela

You will find South Africa still divided by tribe, race, class,
and the shadow of apartheid. Though these are social conditions, they pose commercial risks to aspects of your enterprise.
One response to these risks is to analyze the current enmities
among potential clientele, then modify your project strategy. A
second, perhaps less obvious, is to analyze the origins of these
enmities, which may lie deep within the nation's past. By exploring the history of these conflicts, you may decide to modify
your market focus.

Is Tribalism a Business Risk?

Contemporary tribalism should be factored into your commercial planning. The term *tribalism* is South African English for

tribal or clan conflict. Because of tribalism, in regions dominated by such conflict, promoting your product in one language
may alienate potential clients who use another. Forming part-
nerships with one clan may preclude dealing with others. I know
one Durban township where by merely entering one area I
would be branded as belonging there and, thus, be treated with
hostility by its neighbor. Such feuds may go back decades or
even centuries. Do not ignore them as outside the realm of
business; they can constitute its core.

Constant Conflict

South Africa's tribal enmities go back to its beginnings, when
there was too much competition for too little fertile land. Most
land there is arid. When rain falls, its sheer intensity erodes the
fragile topsoil and washes vital minerals out of what remains.
During the prehistoric era, such land supported neither humans
nor animals for any length of time. To survive, all were forced
into constant movement. Plains game followed the rains, seeking new grass as it grew. Hunters (human, canine, feline) followed grazers. Herders followed their animals. Farmers moved
as they wore out the soil. Thus, early South Africans were migrants. Permanent settlements were possible in scattered, fertile pockets and along the eastern coast, but settlers could always be dislodged by migrants. It was a society forced by scarcity to remain on the move.

The early San, for instance, were migrant hunter-gather-
ers. Small groups established temporary shelters, but they remained only until the veld around them was picked and hunted
clean of edible plants and animals. Then they migrated, following the rain clouds, grass, and game back and forth across
the veld. Each clan had established routes. They had to defend
them, however, from intruding herders or farmers who could
upset the ecology they required to survive. Thus, when threatened, they fought stealthily with tiny bows and arrows tipped
with poison.

The early Khoi were migrant herders, following fat-tailed sheep and long-horned cattle across the veld. They rode oxen, using them as shields in times of war and trading them during periods of peace. Cattle were wealth; the more a clan acquired, the greater its security and status. Since livestock provided a more stable food supply than hunting, the Khoi lived in tribes of several thousand. But they too had to defend established migration routes against intruders, who could seize the flocks and herds they needed to survive. When threatened, they fought with clubs, shields, and nine-foot, fire-hardened spears (Walker 1928).

The early Bantu were herders and farmers and therefore threatening to Khoi and San alike. They came in tens of thousands with their goats, sheep, and cattle, stopping periodically to plant. Their migration was slow, as single clans floated off from tribal mainstreams, drifting aimlessly away in search of grazing. They had three advantages over San and Khoi groups. The Bantu were taller and more numerous, and they tipped their spears with iron. Nonetheless, the San and Khoi defended their migration routes, the former to preserve wildlife, the latter to protect grazing. Bantu clans fought both with these groups and with one another, using seven-foot spears with six-inch iron tips as well as wooden clubs with knobby ends and tiny shields of oxhide (Morris 1966).

Early warfare, however, was governed by universally accepted rules, intended to limit the extent of the conflict. One rule restricted warring to warriors; women, children, and the old were spared. A second left peacemaking to the elders. Young men started conflicts; the elders resolved them.

They fought in ways no different from the ancient Greeks and Trojans. Two war bands would inch toward each other, hurling insults to bolster their courage, while elders, women, and children from both sides yelled encouragement. Single champions would perform a *giya* (war dance) for the opposing side, daring them to attack. Finally both sides would simultaneously hurl spears, then charge with shield and club (or second spear) in hand. After much pushing and shoving, some warriors would fall, and eventually one side would claim victory and the other would retreat with honor, knowing they would fight again. Conflict was constant, if not lethal, and tribal feuds spanned generations as sons replaced fathers in traditional feuds against traditional foes. Unfortunately, these conflicts continue today.

Total War

After 1818 the earlier Bantu traditions of limited conflict were obliterated by one man. His Zulu name was *uShaga* (English: *Shaka*). Born among people chained by tradition, Shaka embraced innovation. He reinvented the spear by breaking the shaft and lengthening the blade, transforming it from a throwing lance into a thrusting weapon like the Roman short sword. He transformed the oxhide shield into an offensive weapon, enlarging it to cover the warrior's entire body and strengthening the edge so it could hook a foe's shield and toss him off balance. He eliminated sandals, forcing his troops to "stamp dance" barefoot through fields strewn with "devil thorns," which would toughen their feet to the point where they could run fifty miles in a day.

Shaka then militarized his own clan, initially forming one *impi* (regiment; plural *izimpi*) of a thousand men. The older, slower men formed the "chest" of an imaginary ox. Their role was to charge the center of an opposing battle line. Two younger, swifter regiments formed the "horns." Their role was to "gore" (envelop) an enemy from both sides as the chest advanced. The "loins," men of middle age, sat in reserve. The discipline of these izimpi surpasses anything achieved in modern times:

> Over 7,000 Zulus sprang to their feet. "Bayete,"
> they roared. Down crashed 7,000 right feet,
> making the earth shake. Then, the human tidal
> wave swept down in uncanny silence, on a
> 2,000-yard front, in perfect lines of 1,000 men
> each.… At four spears' throw, the deep majestic

> Zulu war chant rolled like rumbling thunder
> across the valley (while) the speed of the
> warriors slowed to the rhythmic, measured
> jog...of a death dance. At every tenth step there
> was an earthshaking stamp of the right foot,
> carried out (in) unison. At one spear's throw, the
> chant ceased. There was a deadly silence, for the
> time required to take a deep breath. Then, the
> fearful Zulu war cry crashed out: "Si-gi-di" and
> the Zulu charged. (Ritter 1955, 200)

Wooden clubs and throwing spears proved useless against this level of regimentation. However, Shaka's innovations were not restricted to the battlefield. After the opposing men had fallen, his izimpi turned on the watching elders, women, and children, slaughtering everyone. Thereafter, they scourged the enemy land, seizing livestock and burning crops. There were always survivors—but none who forgot or forgave. Too often, their descendants still view contemporary Zulu as their tribal enemy.

Mutual Extermination

Contemporary tribal discord is also rooted in memories of mutual extermination. In the 1820s, Shaka's killing machine raged in all directions. Deprived within hours of livestock, women, and children, non-Zulu survivors of the carnage saw no alternative but to adopt Zulu tactics themselves. Starving regiments of refugees fell upon more distant groups, to savage them in turn. Those who survived regrouped and attacked others. The waves of mass madness spread outward in every direction, inundating the veld.

Nguni and Sotho alike recall this period as *iMfecane,* "The [time of] Crushing." The exterminators swept south among the coastal Xhosa, north to the Swazi, and east over the High Veld. The KhoiSan died or fled into the Dragon Mountains. The entire Sotho social structure collapsed. Opposing Zulu clans fled hundreds of miles to avoid Shaka's wrath. Survivors turned to cannibalism. Others evolved into migrating scavengers, killing whomever they met, then living off the victims' meager supplies. Whole regions became blackened wastelands, inhabited only by starving, maddened wanderers. Indeed, the first Whites to enter the High Veld found no trace of life except for unending heaps of skeletons, which their wooden wagon wheels crushed as they passed.

In time, the scattered tribes re-formed. Nonetheless, decades of mutual extermination had done its work. Tribal, clan, and even family hatreds were now deeply rooted across the land and transferred to each new generation by the tales passed around the evening fires. The Zulu and Xhosa, among others, turned their hatred inward, creating interclan vendettas that still endure.

Contemporary clansmen still carry on the ancient feuds. Teenage boys, in multitribal urban settings, still gather for "faction fights": Zulu against Tswana against Xhosa against Sotho. Each boy is armed with two fighting sticks; they fight in shoving, shrieking groups until one side retreats. The scene recurs among adults, where workers from contending labor hostels still square off along tribal lines, well armed with fighting sticks and spears. Indeed, entire hostels in today's Gauteng, each preempted by one tribe, wage war on other hostels with Kalashnikov assault rifles.

In KwaZulu-Natal, the feuding is political, the fighting intratribal. Here, members of the African National Congress (ANC) and Inkatha Freedom Party, all Zulu, stalk and kill each other (Drogin 1996). Some groups keep count, noting which clans owe them bodies and how many. Others hire *amashinga* (assassins) to ensure that they stay ahead in the number killed (Taylor 1994). Tribal, clan, and even family members who would normally regard one another as kin are still estranged from each other by old antagonisms that will not die.

In these settings tribalism can indeed become a business problem. It can alter your first decisions as to where you locate and with whom you deal. Sometimes tribal enmity can prove useful. Marketing within a hostile climate forces you to focus on people, putting your product mentally aside to learn what is happening in your projected market, to whom, and why.

Tribal conflicts may force you to take sides. That can also be useful. Joining one group can provide introductions to their allies. Hiring from among traditionally friendly (rather than hostile) factions may lower workplace strife. Successful promotions in one region may work in others, occupied by related clans. Americans joke that success is not what but whom you know. Among Africans, that proverb is no joke. It is how you do business.

Is White "Racialism" a Business Risk?

The problems raised by white racialism should also be factored into your initial planning. The word *racialism*, as explained earlier, is South African English for "racial hostility." Both black and white racialism run strong in South Africa. Each springs from fear of the other, and both pose risks for foreign business. White animosity goes back four hundred years. It is (and has always been) based on the two fears a small minority always feels about the large majority: war can bring extinction, but peace can mean absorption.

Consider, as a historic example, the specific fears felt by the first small band of Whites to reach South Africa. In 1651, within minutes of first landing at the Cape, eighty Dutch men, six women, and twelve children were confronted by three distinct tribes of Khoi (Gorinhaikonas, Gorinhaiquas, Gorachoquas), totaling 918 spear-bearing warriors (Walker). The Dutch had guns, but in the 1650s one could never be sure they would actually fire (Elphick 1985). Jan Van Riebeeck, their leader, soon learned there were at least seven other "savage" groups nearby. Hopelessly outnumbered, he faced three choices—the same three options that outnumbered white minorities would face for the next four hundred years: full integration, geographic partition, or social separation (apartheid).

Van Riebeeck first chose peace and with it, integration. Once safely back on shipboard, he ordered any Dutchman who ill-treated, beat, or even pushed a native to receive fifty lashes, so that everyone might know they came in peace (Walker). This first choice foundered on the rocks of intercultural conflict. Then, as now, Europeans and Africans had different visions as to the use of material goods, livestock, women, and land. The Khoi felt that all things—from the ship's tools to grazing land and water—should be shared. The Dutch believed that private ownership (including land, grazing, and water) meant excluding others. The Khoi sought Dutch possessions. The Dutch sought Khoi land, water, livestock, and women. Conflicting visions led to war. The integration option was a failure.

Van Riebeeck's second option was partition. Each time the Dutch waged war, they won and advanced inland. The Khoi retreated into the interior to recruit additional allies and fight again. As a result, each *victory decreased* white feelings of security. They gained new land and livestock to protect, while Khoi hostility intensified with each defeat. Consequently, after one such empty victory, Van Riebeeck tried partition. He separated Dutch and Khoi by building a barrier of guard posts and planting thorny bitter almond hedges in between them, to form a nine-mile-long half-circle around the colony (Walker).

This second option also failed for the same reason that each attempt at partition would fail in the future. Van Riebeeck's hedge was trampled down by Khoi and Dutch alike, since the more each learned of the other, the more interdependent they became. Dutchmen slipped out through the barrier, bent on obtaining Khoi livestock and women. Khoi slipped in, equally desirous of Dutch cloth, iron, tobacco, and rum (Elphick). To Dutch authorities, this meant the enemy was now within the walls, a problem that intensified with the subsequent arrival of "other natives"—actually Dutch slaves, seized in West Africa and the East Indies.

All the natives within Van Riebeeck's wall caused the Dutch intense anxiety. "Bad" Khoi stole as often as they traded. "Bad"

West Africans and East Indians (Malays) shirked work, escaped, or ran amok, killing everyone they met until they themselves were killed. As nonwhites multiplied around them, Whites' fears of uprising and thus extinction intensified.

Conversely, "good" natives worried the Dutch by cooperating. Some became Christian; some became wives; others become mistresses, then mothers of Dutch children. Many learned Dutch skills so well they grew rich. One Cape slave (Anthony van Angola) became Christian, bought his freedom, obtained land, and bought another slave to work it. Thereafter, he purchased 154 sheep, 1 horse, and 14 oxen (Curtin 1969). For the Dutch, this type of behavior raised the specter of dilution. If nonwhites could have access to Dutch baptism, wealth, status, marriage, and subsequent parentage, white culture might dilute and eventually disappear.

Faced with this dilemma, the Dutch (and their Afrikaner descendants) chose the third option: a society that combined physical domination, economic monopoly, and social separation. Later, they would call this system "apartheid." Initially, this meant closing off existing paths to equality. Christianity was reinterpreted to portray Whites as people chosen by God to rule others. Slave baptisms died away, while religious instruction shrank to attendance at prayer. Racial intermarriage and concubinage vanished when orphanages in the Netherlands provided settler wives. Nonwhites were gradually forbidden to acquire wealth in any form. They were also forbidden to learn or even speak formal Dutch and were compelled instead to address Whites in dialect. Even speaking as equals was forbidden, as nonwhites were forced to adopt physical and vocal mannerisms (cringing, whining, etc.) that exaggerated and caricatured servility.

This third option succeeded. The Khoi, for example, first lost all their livestock, then all their lands, and finally even their social structure when European diseases swept inland from the Cape to decimate them. The shattered remnants, now permanently addicted to Europe's material goods, accepted slave status among Dutch families. The master/slave mentality that emerged among Whites was subsequently extended to other groups and eventually to the Bantu. It has continued up to modern times.

Is Black Racialism a Business Risk?

Black racialism, hostility toward Whites, should also be factored into your project planning. Like its white counterpart, black racialism is based on two related fears: economic exploitation and social degradation. The roots of these fears also go back four hundred years. One of the oldest is fear for their land—which Europeans had virtually seized at will from the time they arrived.

Land Seizure

As the Dutch moved away from the Cape, they seized land as they went. Blocked by desert in the west and arid mountains to the north, Cape Dutch settlers first edged timidly eastward along the coastline, expanding one hunting zone, grassland, or farm at a time. Initially, their hunters left settled areas to seek and subsequently decimate wild game. Trekboers followed them, seizing grazing land and water sources. Boer farmers followed, claiming six thousand hectare tracts per man. By the 1760s all former KhoiSan land was white owned. In the 1770s the first of these migrants found their eastward migration route blocked by the far more numerous Xhosa. Six decades of stalemated warfare followed as both sides raided livestock, but neither yielded land.

In the 1830s frontier trekboers began what is still known as "The Great Trek," migrating inland over the mountains and onto the sparsely populated High Veld, thereby avoiding the Xhosa completely. They lived in covered wagons, which they dismantled each time they crossed a mountain, then reassembled on level veld. The pace was that of a plodding ox team; the stops were decided by a team's need to graze.

Over time, the migrants lost much of their European heritage. They became illiterate from years of reading only from a Bible. Lacking water, they rarely bathed. Always moving, they devalued material goods, keeping only what their wagons could carry. Cattle became their currency and the measure of their wealth. In short, they adapted to the High Veld exactly as had the Bantu before them, evolving into slowly moving clans of nomad herders.

They did retain three aspects of their Western past. One was their dependence on coffee, sugar, and tobacco. A second was the belief that as God's chosen people, they deserved service from other peoples. The third was their mastery of the gun. In Europe weapons technology had continued to evolve, so that the guns available to voortrekkers by the 1830s were more reliable and accurate than those used by Van Riebeeck in the 1650s. Moreover, ten generations of ceaseless hunting had honed trekboer marksmanship to the point where their concentrated fire could be devastating.

In contrast, neither Bantu tactics nor weapons advanced beyond those developed by Shaka. In theory, his combination of regimental discipline and overwhelming numbers should have made the Bantu invincible. In fact, the Whites developed two countertactics that eventually enabled them to conquer the entire veld.

When threatened, they "went into *laager*" (fortification), lashing their wagons together in tight circles, then filling the gaps with thornbush. Men fired through the thorns, women reloaded. Thus sheltered, they could fire continuously for the few hours required for attackers to grow hungry, thirsty, and exhausted, since Bantu carried little food and water to war. As the attackers withdrew, the trekboers gave chase on horseback, riding in two ranks. If the warriors rallied, the white front rank dismounted, fired in unison, remounted, galloped to the rear, and reloaded. Then, the second rank dismounted, fired in unison, and repeated the process. If threatened, these alternating ranks could simply ride beyond the range of running Bantu. If advancing, they could catch and trample the swiftest warrior, whose only defense was an upward thrust with his shortened spear.

The clearest test of both trekboer and Bantu tactics came in 1836, when a wave of trekboers met the six thousand-man Zulu impi of Mzilikazi, once Shaka's most effective general. The two sides fought three times, the last for nine days (Laband 1995). The Zulu attacked and reattacked the White laager in perfect formation. Each time, the wagons held, the impi fell back, and the trekboers rode out to shoot them down. Finally the Zulu faltered, then they were driven from the field and eventually from the High Veld. Their defeat foreshadowed the future conquest of every Bantu group in Southern Africa.

When the Whites conquered, however, they seized not merely cattle (as would the Bantu, had they won) but the land itself. Over time, the sheer scope of these seizures reached extraordinary heights. During the 1700s land seized from Khoi herders was allotted to Cape Dutch immigrants at six thousand hectares per man. During the 1800s land-hungry British migrants entered the region, followed by British armies. On defeating the Zulu in the 1840s, Britain eventually gave four thousand square miles of its kingdom to the Boers, took 40 percent of what remained, and nibbled for the next twenty years at what fragments the Zulu still held (Taylor). By 1904 eight thousand Whites owned six million acres. Each Zulu owned, on average, less than two.

In practical terms this meant that Zulu clans found themselves jammed into ever shrinking slices of terrain, caught between newly white-owned farms, forests, grazing lands, and mountains—to which access was now legally forbidden. For nine decades thereafter, *no* Zulu land was safe from seizure. Any White could reduce any Zulu to poverty by legal dispossession. Such memories do not die. Whites still hold much of that land, while the African landless still hunger for what was once theirs.

Exploitation of Labor

Black racialism is also based on the fear, despite The Turn, that Whites will continue to exploit their labor. This belief also goes back decades, to the time when, after each military conquest, so few Whites received so much land that none could effectively work it. A single farmer might acquire thousands of High Veld acres, but much of it was waterless. The short, erratic rainy season dictated that plowing, sowing, and reaping had to begin with little warning and at fever pitch, before the earth once more baked dry. Thus, a man wishing to plow 20,000 arid acres had to find 20 plows, 280 oxen, 60 men to control them, and 100 others to plant (Keegan 1983). In short, having seized too much land to work themselves, white farmers needed free labor to farm it.

European farmers first moved against those African clans who still lived on the lands the Whites had just acquired. Up to this time these families had consumed milk and meat from their livestock; gathered wild fruit and honey; and raised mealies (corn), pumpkins, and beans on small plots near their homes. In short, they were independent herder/farmers.

Their first shock must have come on learning that the land, which they believed all men held in common, now belonged to a single European. The second, no doubt, came when they learned that to stay on that land, each household must pay rent. The Whites had previously seized their livestock. Owning nothing else with which to pay, they were obliged to labor. By so doing, they were transformed from independent herder/farmers into part-time sharecroppers—half slave, half free—working both white acreage and plots still assigned them as their own (Keegan).

Over time, the Whites developed ways to exploit the sharecroppers more efficiently. Some Africans worked their allotted plots well enough to create surpluses for sale. This cash made tenants less dependent on their landlords and less willing to labor on demand. As a result, Whites passed laws forbidding rent payments in cash or produce; they required farm labor instead. Thereafter, Blacks who sought more independence through effective farming were evicted for "refusing to work." Those remaining were transformed once more, from sharecroppers to unpaid squatters.

Whites then extended the squatter system into serfdom. Laws redefined black wage earners as "servants," thereby legalizing punishment both for evading work *and* for insufficient servility. Then, the term *servant* was extended to black wives and children, enabling newly designated "masters" to require their services as well. Thereafter, wages could be paid in food (or milk) instead of cash. Soon, Africans were stripped of both legal defenses and hope. Men who began life as independent herder/farmers left it as serfs and the fathers of serfs.

Whites then moved against those Africans living beyond their farms in the newly designated "native reserves," into which, you will recall, entire tribes were herded after their military defeat. Initially, European farmers tried to lure men out of these reserves by offering trade goods. This led to Africans working until they received the promised goods, then leaving white employment forever. Worse, during the brief, frantic plowing and harvesting periods, they worked only their own land, simply ignoring European pleas.

White authorities responded by ruling that "Location Africans" must be taxed. To earn the tax, each man had to labor for a landholder. Initially, a tax was levied on each hut. The Africans destroyed most of their huts and moved in together. Then taxes were levied on dogs, beads, marriage, and, finally, adult males. The Europeans, of course, had related goals: to gradually induce bankruptcy and compel the suddenly impoverished Africans to labor under any conditions they imposed. They succeeded.

> Defeated dislocated and confused…the descendants of those who had marched with
> Shaka…came to the White man's doors, wary
> and polite…donning the khaki shorts and tunic
> of a "houseboy" and meekly submitting to the
> haranguing of an overbearing white madam.
> (Taylor, 267)

Noncompliance was crushed. In Natal colony, for example, the constant demand for African workers had created the *isibalo* (forced labor system) that required white-appointed "chiefs" to supply a stipulated number of unpaid workers on demand. When one Zulu clan head refused in 1906, his people were surrounded and shelled with artillery. When another clan fled into a forest, they were slaughtered with dumdum bullets. The terrified survivors were then stripped of *all* their assets. All crops were burned, all livestock seized, and all remaining land put up "for sale to white men" (Taylor). In these two cases alone, thirty thousand people were made homeless, rendered paupers, and forced into serfdom.

Every clan history records similar instances. Indeed, the three-step process of land dispossession, goods expropriation, and labor exploitation was universal. Such levels of physical suffering and social degradation are not forgotten. They form the roots of today's black racialism. You may therefore wish to reshape both your personal and project strategy to deal with this racist reality.

Is Apartheid a Business Risk ?

The legacy of apartheid must also be considered in your business planning. *Apartheid* means "apartness" in Afrikaans. It was originally conceived of as the most certain way for each culture in a multicultural society to both preserve its individual identity and live in peace. Racial peace was felt to depend on each race developing in isolation, whereas continued contact would create unending racial conflict.

The system officially began in 1948. In fact, the apartheid laws simply codified earlier traditions in use since the Cape Dutch first segregated themselves from KhoiSan, Malay, and African slaves. From an economic perspective, the system was based on the European desire to maximize profit by guaranteeing labor supply and minimizing labor costs. Thus, geographic and social separation were combined with economic exploitation.

Apartheid ended legally in 1991. Nonetheless, it still exists. Although the races mingle in daylight, most resegregate at sunset, returning to single-race neighborhoods. African elitists still protest that white business excludes them. African workers still feel that white bosses exploit them. Black consumers still bypass stores, bars, and entire shopping centers they perceive as "White." White consumers ignore those they view as "Black." In short, the system is illegal, but still alive. It seems prudent, therefore, to shape commercial strategy to this segregated reality.

Apartheid originally had five economic goals, each meant to transform the nonwhite population into a "Permanent Underpaid Labor Pool" (PULP). The first step was to identify and racially classify those from whom low-cost labor was desired. Classification was based on ancestry, appearance, reputation, and how others classified you. Once labeled, people were to live in areas assigned to their racial group. They could not marry, have sexual relations, or display public affection with anyone outside their group. They were restricted to jobs allotted that group and subject to laws devised for it. Spouses classified separately were to divorce and live in separate areas. Parents and children classified separately were to separate. This stage of apartheid succeeded. It proved possible to identify, register, classify, and segregate the nonwhite population into a PULP.

Rural Labor Exploitation

The second step was to economically exploit the rural PULP. By 1913, 70 percent of the South Africans had been forced into scattered tribal locations ("homelands"), covering only 13 percent of the land. The founders of apartheid knew these areas could not economically support such numbers. They therefore decided to force the men to leave the homelands and seek work elsewhere.

Each homeland was to be ringed with white farms (or factories), with European towns nearby. Workers could be transported to work sites at dawn, made to labor until dusk, then returned to the homeland at night. Alternatively, the homelands, or reserves, themselves could be moved en masse and their entire populations regrouped around white industrial zones. This would maximize black employment while minimizing both white transport costs and wages. The goal, of course, was to separate all Bantu from the land, thereby transforming them from independent subsistence farmers into industrial proletarians.

Urban Labor Exploitation

The third step was to move all urban Africans out of the cities into native townships, located miles from each urban core. Police often bulldozed their former homes, destroying furnishings, places of worship, gardens, trees, work tools, and communal structures (Mayibuye 1996). The residents were then trucked to arid open areas and resettled in rows of tiny, simple, identical dwellings that could extend for miles. The government provided water and food for purchase. It did not provide electricity, bars, cinemas, restaurants, nightclubs, and the other amenities that can combine to create a vibrant urban core.

Each African attempt to create such amenities was ruled illegal and replaced by white monopolies. For instance, efforts by Bantu women to brew traditional beers were first officially forbidden, then replaced by white-operated beer halls. Nor did the government provide trees, fountains, or anything else to create a pleasant living area. Instead, the urban townships remained, as their founders intended, nothing more than massive dormitories for the PULP.

The fourth step was to control the movement of this urban PULP between residence and work. That meant requiring each adult African to carry a "pass" (identity book). The book held permits meant to control the holder's every move. One permit required him to live in a location; another let him board one bus to work and the same bus back to the township. A third permitted work for a specific European. Consequently, the holder of each pass could be at home, en route, or at work—nowhere else.

To visit outside one's location required a visiting pass. To buy a goat required a purchase pass. To visit husbands in urban locations for forty-eight hours, rural wives were required to obtain a conjugal pass. To stay a month, they needed a conception pass.

Since each permit was issued by a White, acquiring one meant demeaning oneself by displaying sufficient servility. Consider the shame for a black woman asking white officials' permission to conceive a child or for grandfathers, fathers, and male teenagers seeking passes to leave a reserve, forced to stand naked in rows until a white doctor inspected their genitals. "Vula! (Open!). [The command] thunders into the man's surprised face. Looking down…he shamefully presents his intimates to the white man" (Klasste 1984, C2–C3).

To receive a pass, Africans had to be judged both "clean" (disease free) *and* sufficiently servile. Each attempt to use the pass required additional displays of servility. To leave a location required servility before the white location *baas* (boss). To board a bus required servility to the white driver baas. To keep a job required servility to white employers, their wives, and their children, since they could all destroy a pass at whim. That loss might mean prison. White police could demand the pass of any African at any time. Failure to produce it could mean up to two years of unpaid prison labor, often on white farms. In social terms, the system was intended to impose the additional burden of behavioral servility ("displaying respect") on a militarily defeated population. Commercially, it was meant to permanently regulate the movement of African PULP.

Social Regulation

The fifth and final step was meant to regulate the African mind. One method was to bar access to "outsiders," whether foreign or urban. The PULP would remain in an idealized (tribal) stage of existence. One way to achieve this was to forbid access to urban life, particularly urban amenities. As a result, "Whites only" signs appeared wherever people of different races might congregate and talk. Cinemas, beaches, parks, restaurants, and elevators were marked "Whites only," as were taxi stands, bus stops, libraries, and lawns. Besides reserving these things for Europeans, the secondary goal was to inhibit even casual interracial conversation and the exchange of ideas that could upset the status quo.

Bantu education was also reshaped to restrict intellectual access to outside influences. The language of instruction was either tribal or Afrikaans, excluding English with its focus on personal freedom. Curricula were limited to skills required for menial labor. From primary school to university, lessons were systematically simplified to the point of utter boredom for the students, on the assumption that the learners could barely learn. Once, during the apartheid years, I watched a class in janitorial training. The act of sweeping had been broken into ten separate steps, which students practiced in unison until stupefied. The stated goal was to "train Bantu only to respond to…simple instructions from their masters" (Olmstead 1985). The unstated goal was to raise children to replace parents at the bottom levels of society and to accept their fate as PULP.

Commercial Lessons from the Past

You have one overriding commercial reason to examine South Africa's tribal and racial history. It is because these deep-rooted enmities are *not* merely history but are part of this nation's contemporary life. You must therefore begin your operations within an atmosphere of multifaceted mistrust. Whether this becomes a business problem depends, in part, on how you are initially perceived. Consider the relationships you plan to form with current African elites. What do they remember from the past? Black medical graduates at the University of Natal still recall that they were

> not allowed on campus, not allowed to use its
> library, not allowed [to play] sport…not allowed
> to wear the University blazer…[as well as] a
> lecturer who forced a first-year African medical
> student to shout "I'm a monkey" to the whole
> class. (*Focus* 1966, 15)

Nor are such experiences simply history. Consider this letter from someone lower on the social scale:

> My mother works as a domestic for a [white]
> farmer. We are not paid...but the farmer gives
> us...food...and milk.... What worries me is that
> he beats us if we don't work...and calls us lazy
> klein kaffirs. He threatens to kick us...[off the
> farm] and tells us we will starve. (Sibiya 1996, 6)

This letter appeared in a South African newspaper in 1996, not 1896. Is it an exception? I experienced similar instances in 1996, where Whites displayed striking discourtesy to Blacks. In one European home the Sotho servants ate standing, facing a wall, while Whites ate together at the table. In another, the Zulu maid was forbidden to eat from the spoons of her employer and told to bring one from home to use when eating. I often passed a white farmer driving his truck in the rain. His dog rode in the cab; the black employee rode outside in the back. I shopped at a convenience store where I would hand money to the black clerk only to see him pass it to a white clerk, who alone could drop it in the cash drawer. None of those Whites (when asked) felt they were racialist. The Blacks (when asked) not only felt they were, but expected nothing else: "In any case, all whites, I dare say, with very, very, very few exceptions, have been socialized into racism" (Shongwe 1996).

It is therefore not merely possible but probable that your initial African contacts may expect you to carry on the exploitation they have known all their lives. Such feelings are most likely to appear if you use U.S. marketing approaches that focus solely on a product. What seems effective to us may look exploitative to them. Use African methods instead, and form personal rather than product relationships. One way to combat both tribal and racial hostility is to begin your business venture by marketing yourself.

References

Curtin, Philip. Professor, Comparative Tropical History, University of Wisconsin. 1969. Personal communication with author.

Drogin, Bob. 1996. "S. Africa's Part-Time President." *Los Angeles Times* (16 September).

Elphick, Richard. 1985. *Khoikhoi and the Founding of White South Africa*. Johannesburg: Ravan Press, 44, 73, 89, 96–99.

Focus. 1966. "Now a New Beginning." Royal University of Natal 7, no. 2, 15–16.

Keegan, Tim. 1983. "The Sharecropping Economy, African Class Formation and the 1913 Native Land Act in the Highveld Maize Belt." In *Town and Countryside in the Transvaal*, edited by Belinda Bozolli. Johannesburg: Ravan Press, 109–17.

Klasste, Aggrey. 1984. "The Strife for Today's Black South African." *San Francisco Chronicle* (4 July).

Laband, John. 1995. *Rope of Sand: The Rise and Fall of the Zulu Kingdom in the 19th Century*. Johannesburg: Jonathan Ball, 81.

Mandela, Nelson. 1994. *Long Walk to Freedom*. London: Abacus Books, Little, Brown, 172.

Mayibuye: Truth and Reconciliation—A Special Mayibuye Supplement African National Congress, Johannesburg, 1996. "Violence of Forced Removals" (July): 3.

Morris, Donald. 1966. *The Washing of the Spears: The Rise and Fall of the Zulu Nation*. London: Jonathan Cape, 24–37.

Olmstead, Larry. 1985. "Segregation: A South African Way of Life," a six-part series. *Detroit Free Press* (15–21 December).

Ritter, E. A. 1955. *Shaka Zulu, Mentor*. New York: New American Library.

Shongwe, Vusi. 1996. "I Speak My Mind: A Focus on Racism." University of Zululand Bulletin 6, no. 13 (22 August).

Sibiya, Khulu. 1996. "Silent Rules Keep Us Apart." *Mail and Guardian*, Johannesburg (30 July).

Taylor, Stephen. 1994. *Shaka's Children: A History of the Zulu People*. London: HarperCollins, 267, 276–78, 318–20.

Walker, Eric A. 1928. *A History of Southern Africa*. London: Longmanns, Green, 35–41.

3

Predeparture: How to Prepare

My employees don't need to prepare for an
overseas assignment. I can teach them what they
need to know about their work abroad just sitting
in my office.

　　　　　　　　　　　—American CEO, Silicon Valley

Insufficient orientation is the third type of
mistake...corporations make [in sending
American managers abroad]. It is simply not
enough to explain the new country's currency,
reel off statistics about its population and gross
national product and give the departing hero a
restaurant guide.

　　　　　　　　　　　—Frederica Hoge Dunn

Marketing yourself in South African settings will work best if
you prepare before departure. In the frantic final weeks before
actually leaving, that may be hard to do. You will have two
predeparture goals. One is self-sufficiency on arrival, to the
point where you can find transport, lodging, food, and a place
to work. You must therefore decide what to learn before leaving, so that you will feel oriented on landing. The second goal,
as mentioned, is to prepare the groundwork for creating personal ties with the people you will meet. To work commercially with Africans, you must engage them emotionally. So
you must also decide what to learn before leaving in order to
make friends once you arrive.

Make Connections

Begin by using the final weeks before departure to develop three distinct networks of American-based advisers. One should consist of South Africans, white and nonwhite, now living in the United States. A second should include African regional experts—Americans (and other nationalities) with past South African experience. A third should focus on their spouses— who may have different perspectives on everything.

Start this search in your own firm, by asking which colleagues have personal contacts, professional expertise, prior travel, or current interests in South Africa. Next, look for similar advisers in related firms; then move beyond them to seek contacts in related fields. When you locate someone with the experience or expertise you seek, ask him or her to introduce you to others. Seek nationals, ex-nationals (emigrants), expatriates, missionaries, Africanists, South Africanists, and regional Southern African specialists.

Black South Africans now teach and study in U.S. universities. White South Africans now migrate in thousands to the United States. Many band together socially in "Springbok" clubs, using the name of both an African antelope and a beloved rugby team, and can be located through South African consulates. Both black and white South Africans are often homesick, follow national events, will discuss them gladly, and can provide useful advice.

Stay off the phone and away from e-mail. Meet each new contact personally, either formally during business hours or socially over food and drinks. Use your foreign inexperience as a business tool, thereby allowing contacts to teach what *they* feel you should know. Your ultimate goal (beyond acquiring data) should be introductions to people in South Africa itself. At some point, ask each American-based contact to introduce you (by phone, fax, or e-mail from the U.S.) to the *one* South African he or she feels might be most useful to your work. Your contact person, in her or his introduction, should simply ask if you may call for an appointment after you arrive in South Africa in order to seek professional advice. Most people enjoy requests for advice from first-time foreign visitors and will agree.

A few days after the first message has been sent, *you* should phone, fax, or e-mail this South African individual. Your overt goal will be to introduce yourself and thank the person in advance for taking the time to speak with you upon your arrival. Your real purpose, of course, is to ask how you may be of service while you are still in the United States. This offer is important, as you can place future contacts under obligation even before you arrive.

I once made this offer to a Capetonian in South Africa. He responded by asking me to bring a twenty-year-old hand-drawn map to Cape Town. He had created it while a student in the United States but had forgotten it on departure. It was now a segment of his history. I located the map and took it on the plane and delivered it in person. I simply saw a drawing; he saw a record of his youth. He was more than grateful; he proved professionally helpful. That introduction evolved into a lifetime alliance. If each contact at home provides one in South Africa and if you follow up each introduction by offering your services before you leave, you will create a web of South Africans prepared to help once you arrive.

Recent History

Supplement your networking by reading about South Africa's recent past—the years every South African you meet has lived through. Explore Black South Africa's struggle for freedom. One starting point could be Edward Roux's now classic book, *Time Longer than Rope,* which details each early step of the African war against apartheid (1964). Follow this book with ex-President Mandela's book, *Long Walk to Freedom,* which captures the passion of those who united to fight oppression.

> Chief Luthuli…sprang to his feet and began to
> dance…. His movements electrified us and we

> took to our feet and joined in indlamu, the...Zulu
> war dance.... Suddenly, there were no Xhosas or
> Zulus, no Indians or Africans, no rightists or
> leftists. We were all nationalists...bound together
> by a love of our...history, our culture, our
> country, and our people. (1994, 235)

Begin your reading with the 1950s, the decade of danger to everyone born black. South Africa's Africans lived in a brutish world: segregated, exploited, degraded, and oppressed. Earlier decades of nonviolent resistance had failed. Earlier leaders had even petitioned British kings, begging for protection against white-imposed servitude, but nothing changed. Whole tribes fled their homelands to escape labor recruiters. They were rounded up and imprisoned in reserves, where new recruiters then appeared. African religious leaders abandoned traditional gods for Western Christianity, but nothing changed. Secular leaders abandoned tradition altogether and adopted Western ways. Still nothing changed. No one gained equality and everyone remained oppressed.

In the 1950s Africans turned to Gandhi's concept of moral resistance, hoping to at least shame white authorities into lightening their bondage. Township Blacks began to peacefully defy the hated pass laws in ever rising numbers, hoping at first to merely fill the nation's jails in a gentle protest that might soften white hearts. Thousands of violators were arrested and rearrested yearly. Still nothing changed. To intensify the moral pressure, they began to march in the thousands, surrounding white police stations in black townships, burning their passes and demanding that police arrest them all for violating pass laws.

Too often, the police responded with bullets and then with arrests, imprisonment, and torture. By 1965 a generation of African leaders, including Mandela, had been arrested, convicted, and imprisoned. A generation of African marchers had been labeled criminals and lived in terror of the law. The marches continued. The arrests continued. Those released from prison returned to marching. Once again, nothing changed.

Driven finally to violence, a new wave of black leaders decided to "liberate" their townships and locations. By the mid-1970s, they succeeded. Every white-supplied amenity—ambulances, beer halls, clinics, cinemas, even school equipment—went up in flames. Black township officials resigned en masse. Black police fled or hid. Black mayors fled or were killed. By the 1980s increasingly well organized black consumer boycotts began to bankrupt white firms.

Whites fought back, of course. By 1984 a new generation of young Africans had been effectively "criminalized" by over two hundred thousand black arrests each year (Smiley 1986). Young leaders were hunted down, tortured, and often murdered by white assassination squads (Ignatieff 1997). Followers were arrested at random, as white police targeted any black youth they saw. It was a time of terror for every African, particularly the young. As one respected Zulu trader described those years to me:

> Police did not symbolize law, just fear. We woke in fear, ate food in fear, worked in fear and could not sleep for fear. Just to see a white man was to be afraid in our stomachs; like their dogs, we never knew if they would turn on us as we passed by.

To discuss those decades today is to recall a time that Blacks and Whites alike remember well. The danger was not remote—as so often is the case in our American lives—but immediate, intense, and equally terrifying to both sides, for Whites feared Blacks as well. As one Afrikaner woman told me in words hauntingly similar to the Zulu trader's: "You could feel the fear in you as you passed them [Africans]. They would step off the sidewalk for you to let you pass, but you never knew if they would turn on you as you moved on by."

The more you read about these times before your departure, the more perceptively you will discuss them with those you will meet upon arrival. Such inquiries, on your part, are one way to build empathy.

Read, too, about the years of pride. As the 1980s ended, white South Africa was near collapse. The Bantu Homelands moved toward economic standstill. The Zulu waged low-level civil war, marked by daily assassinations. Young Whites grew increasingly opposed to a military draft that swept them into an unending border war against Namibian guerrillas. Africans set off bombs in white shopping centers, communicating their own sense of terror to the enemy. Foreign banks withdrew capital. The rand declined. By 1988–89, the nation faced financial, economic, and social disaster.

In 1989 F. W. de Klerk won a Whites-only election by offering reforms. In 1990 he began to dismantle the apartheid system, first freeing Mandela after twenty-seven years of imprisonment, then ending a thirty-year ban on the ANC. In 1991 he removed apartheid's legal cornerstones: the laws blocking African access to land and cities and the regulations that had restricted social interaction. It was only three years later that Mandela led the ANC to power in a political, economic, and racial transition that proved so peaceful as to amaze the world. These were surely years of pride. You can begin to share them by reading *Tomorrow Is Another Country*, by Allister Sparks (1996).

Relevant Geography

Geographic grounding can both increase your sense of self-sufficiency and help to form new ties. But South African geography books may prove irrelevant to your business needs. Instead, focus your research on the two areas where you first intend to live and work as well as every route between them. To increase your self-sufficiency and safety, examine each for zones of danger. For greater empathy with Africans, seek out their points of pride.

Danger Zones

In parts of South Africa, crime is out of control. One KwaZulu manager now considers Johannesburg to be so dangerous that he flies only to its airport, conducts business in an executive lounge, and then flies home. The management of Johannesburg's once luxurious Carleton Center Hotel, now closed, at one time offered a personal security guard to *each guest* leaving the grounds. In 1996 the ultra-prestigious Rand Club, a private gathering place for South Africa's elite since the discovery of gold, found its membership declining due to the continuous rattle of gunfire at night. By 1999 the level of gunfire had risen to where the club had decided to sell its historic building—but found no buyers (Cadman 1999). Rural areas experience similar problems. My rented home in rural KwaZulu had no fewer than nine locks as well as a "rape gate" of iron bars to further protect the bedroom. No one, black or white, is wholly free of fear.

There are steps you can take before leaving, however, to reduce the risk of crime once you land. One useful predeparture tactic is to identify specific business zones, neighborhoods, and the routes that link them where either you or your future staff might be endangered. One source of such data is East View Publications, a Minneapolis map supplier to the United States Library of Congress. It can provide maps that are accurate to the point of showing single dwellings (Petzinger 1998).

Show these maps to South African contacts from every major ethnic group. Initially, ask them to look at the areas you are considering for the location of your headquarters and to divide them into those they consider dangerous, borderline, and safe. Then ask them to explain why. White, Black, and Asian South Africans may provide sharply different answers. Nonetheless, patterns do appear. If sixteen people suggest that Durban's seafront is dangerous while three consider it safe, you have a basis on which to make decisions.

Next, ask your contacts to look at the neighborhoods in which you may decide to live. Inquire as to their safety—by day and by night. Then, ask if the routes you plan to drive between work and home are safe (by day and by night) from carjacking; if not, what other routes exist and at what hours are they safest? What about parking? Are driveways safe from car-jackers? If not, must you hire security guards? If so, from which clans, and how much should you pay?

Finally, expand your inquiries to include areas from which you hope to draw potential clients—within a city, adjacent townships, or surrounding countryside. Do tsotsi gangs operate within these zones? Which forms of public transport are considered safe: taxis, minivans, buses, trains? If there are problems with tsotsis, find out when and how and where. You may not plan to use public transportation, but the African staff you hire will. Their safety may depend on your inquiry.

Points of Pride

Your geographic research should also include all African points of pride: historic, architectural, artistic, and environmental. To ignore these achievements because you have come on business will likely prove counterproductive. Conversely, researching them may lead to the personal relationships that become commercial ones.

I learned this from a Zulu colleague, whom I initially found rather dull. I believe he felt the same about me. By chance, he spoke of a battlefield at a hill called *Islandlwana,* where Zulu regiments had decimated an entire British column in 1879. Because I had read briefly of the battle before departure, I said that I would like someday to see the site. He invited me instantly, though it meant a three-hour drive on rough rural roads, plus an hour's scorching climb across the slope.

At first, I saw stones and gullies and sun and sand. He saw whole columns of racing, chanting warriors, sweeping through a single crack in the traditional British military square to slaughter those within. As we climbed and he told the tale, I began to see them too, and the entire era came alive in my mind. On our return trip, the hours of car chat shifted quickly away from business and toward learning more about each other. A little geographic research and one request to see a stony hill transformed a business contact into my teacher and, thereafter, into a mentor and friend.

Learn about Their Leisure

Americans use the phrase "business is business," and separate work in their minds from leisure. Among Africans business begins in leisure hours, when people form relationships. When you arrive in South Africa, you will want to use your leisure time to do the same. Your earliest African contacts may be local elites, who take pride in contemporary aspects of their culture. They may be agreeably surprised if you have learned enough about these interests before landing to be able to discuss them over drinks. But to share such interests, you must develop an interest. What better time to do this than in the weeks before you leave?

One aspect of current South African culture is the "pop" scene. Pop music, art, and theater are partially dominated by American performers. Thus, everyone you meet may know enough about American artists to share a conversation. But why not respond in kind by learning something of their culture heroes while still in the United States?

U.S. theaters now stage plays by South African dramatists such as Athol Fugard *(Valley Song),* Winston Ntshona and John Kani *(Sizwe Banzi Is Dead),* and Mbongeni Ngema *(Serafina).* South African music is also well known. Miriam Makeba, Hugh Masekela, and Ladysmith Black Mambazo are world class, and the Soweto String Quartet blends Europe's classical music with that of modern Africa. Attend their performances and look for their CDs before you go.

Writers from many lands have written lovingly about South Africa, telling their tales in both fact and fiction. As a business professional, perennially short of time, I vote for fiction. Not only can you learn far more in much less time, but you will more likely remember it, if only for the beauty of the words. Start with James A. Michener's magnificent work of historical fiction, *The Covenant,* which depicts the entire sweep of South Africa's history from the San to modern times. Follow it with Peter Abrahams' *Wild Conquest,* which narrows the historical saga to the struggle between Afrikaner and African. South Africa's Alan Paton became world famous for his *Cry, the Beloved Country*. Next, read his less well known *Too Late the Phalerope*, which deals with the topic (then forbidden in South Africa) of interracial love. *Mine Boy*, again by Peter Abrahams, and *Blanket Boy*, by Peter Lanham and A. S. Mopeli-Paulus, will introduce you to contemporary Zulu and Sotho people as they leave their homelands to seek work in the white-owned gold mines. Finally, Percy Fitzpatrick's *Jock of the Bushveld* will introduce you to South Africa's Bushveld at a time when it was almost overrun with wildlife. Told from the perspective of a dog, the tale is as beloved in South Africa as *Lassie Come Home* is in Scotland. There are scores of other world-class writers; I have only suggested those that I love.

Learn something of sports-mad South Africa. In the past, Whites played rugby; Indians, cricket; Africans, soccer. Nowadays, racial lines have faded, and televised matches turn spectators of every color into fans. When South Africa's rugby teams play, the country simply stops. When its cricket teams play in Australia or Fiji, middle-aged matrons turn on the TV at 4:00 A.M.

Since few of us play their sports, Americans are initially at a disadvantage. One predeparture suggestion is simply to ask South African contacts how their games are played. I did this once with a Durbanite. I agreed to explain baseball, using no U.S. slang, and he tried to explain cricket, using no South African slang—more difficult than you might think! Nonetheless, his explanation piqued my interest. Now, if I am invited to watch a cricket match, I not only go but can discuss it (almost) knowledgeably with my hosts. In such settings, even sports can be a business tool.

Indeed, South African sports, music, drama, literature, art, and every other form of leisure can become business tools, if only because they illustrate our interest in their country. If commercial alliances are based on trust, that trust is partially formed by sharing values—including leisure values. Business discussions all too often lead to verbal conflict; so do discussions of race, politics, or economics. In contrast, sports, music, and art reflect human achievements that people of all nations enjoy.

Learn (a Little) Language

I mentioned earlier that learning even a little of an African language suggests that you intend to build ties. Most Americans will agree—but only in theory. We all want to learn "a little" of whatever they speak where we are going. In fact, few of us find time to learn anything at all. The weeks between receiving the assignment and actual departure are too crowded. Nonetheless, even making a beginning in Sotho, Xhosa, or Zulu will prove a useful business tactic. South Africa's white managers now take language training. T.A.L.K., a firm teaching Zulu in Johannesburg, has run fifty courses in the past three years for South African corporations. A competitor now teaches a course entitled "Zulu for Executives" (*Economist* 1996). By undertaking African language training, you honor African culture, thus sending a signal to those Africans with whom you will deal.

I learned this while flying overseas. My frantic days before departure were spent winding up American affairs instead of learning language. Only on the plane did I pull out a phrase book. Two hundred phrases later, I was thoroughly bored but labored dully on. Yet, that evening, I managed to shyly order dinner, respond to verbal kindnesses, and even ask some questions in the local language. My hosts were amused but also impressed. Joking, they asked if I was, in fact, a real American, since none had ever tried to learn their language. Surely my efforts, however unpolished, helped me to market myself.

Very few managers start language study en route, but fewer still begin at home. Taking foreign language classes can unfortunately waste your time. Too many teachers teach what the textbooks dictate, not what businesspeople need. Time is wasted learning words that you will never use.

Nor do foreign language tapes help much. The people who make them want you to read the workbooks they sell with each set of tapes. Since most of us can't spare the time to read, we only play the tapes in our cars. This means the tapes must provide both foreign expressions *and* English translations. Some tapes, however, omit the English. Some introduce words that no one needs, and most pronounce the foreign phrases so quickly (and only once) that the speeding, tired, traffic-harried commuter is soon frustrated. Thus, enthusiasm erodes and the project is doomed by the end of the first tape.

One enjoyable way to learn a South African language is to hire a foreign national as a language informant. To find one, ask at major universities, especially those that offer less commonly taught foreign languages. This is not like hiring a tutor. In fact, you must furiously resist each attempt by the language informant to become a tutor (they always try). Tutors teach what *they* think you should learn; the informant just answers your questions. That means you must ask questions, requesting translations, variations, and explanations of just those words and phrases you feel you need for *your* assignment.

To ask questions, however, you must do your homework by trying to analyze each stage of your project to decide which phrases you might use most often. This individual should not only respond to your questions but also provide context for each one, suggesting not just what to say but how, when, and to whom to say it. Hidden meanings, double meanings, slang equivalents, and offensive (e.g., racist, sexual) variants are vitally important. Inquire too about body language, accent, intonation, and pitch. Americans, for example, have been trained to quote prices loudly (and proudly), thereby suggesting they believe in them. Africans are trained to say them softly, so as to minimize their impact on the hearer. Discussions about such topics can be far more interesting and useful than plodding through a language text.

Supplement this training with a language phrase book and small dictionary. You can order Zulu, Xhosa, and Sotho phrase books through travel bookstores or the Internet. Once you have them, four suggestions may help those of you with great determination but little time:

1. Memorize whole phrases and expressions, rather than lists of isolated words. Lists bore us because they lack context and we forget them.
2. Break up each phrase; then relearn the most useful words. Thus, sentences such as "That hotel is very far away," "Their restaurant is very good," and "The neighborhood seems very safe" should first be memorized in their entirety. Then relearn *very,* since it will recur.
3. Learn only those phrases you might actually use. Most of us ignore 85 percent of a restaurant menu, for instance, to choose among favored foods and drinks.
4. Learn only those questions you might actually ask. Each time you learn one, memorize the most probable answers. "Where is the hotel?" should be learned with *left, right, straight ahead*, and so on.

One further suggestion for predeparture study may prove especially useful as soon as you arrive: African greetings. Learn *every* variation as well as the proper responses. We North Americans greet briefly. Africans greet elaborately, formally honoring the status of everyone involved. A proper greeting (as compared to a one-word tourist greeting) must therefore reflect and honor the age, sex, and status of those greeted. Thus, the greeting you give an unmarried Zulu girl ("I see you, girl") and an older woman ("I see you, mother of _____") will differ. To ignore the status differences may be unintentionally insulting. To respect them confers honor on you.

Your goal is not to display linguistic expertise but an appropriate level of respect. This can be done most artfully by using Zulu, Sotho, or Xhosa to express the minor courtesies that facilitate our daily interactions: salutations and farewells, apologies, gratitude, appreciation, and delight. These are not difficult to learn in any Bantu language, and you will know you are progressing when you see the smiles.

Choose Gifts

Your final task before departure should be to select gifts for those contacts you feel might become colleagues. Choose with care. In South Africa gifts are specifically meant to go beyond generating good feelings to lay a foundation for commercial relationships. Gifts do create empathy, but they are often expected at specific times in each business transaction. Thus, an outsider seeking entry into a specific regional market will often present local authorities with appropriate gifts *before, during,* and *after* doing business. We might call this bribery; they call it tradition.

The first gift signals that the outsider both seeks help and hopes for good relations with the recipient. Subsequent gifts signal the wish to nurture the relationship. Gifts given once business is complete reflect the desire to work together again should an opportunity occur.

Since gift giving forms so great a part of commerce in black South African culture, choose items (or services) that maximize your social and commercial impact. What gift, for instance, can be shared on a festive occasion? On one trip to Swaziland, I brought my host a precooked, honey-baked ham. He responded by throwing a party for me, using my ham as the centerpiece, adding local meat, and inviting everyone he wanted me to know. That evening kick-started my Swazi career, but I simply did what was expected of an honored guest. I contributed to the feast.

Alternatively, consider what gift (or service) might enhance your contact's work. Try a high-tech option. One key contact might appreciate updated software. Another may like a "smart" key that unlocks doors on command or an electronic mosquito repeller. One of my contacts is visually impaired; his gift, a talking watch.

Try a low-tech option. All Africans want to improve their English. I almost gave one contact ten English language tapes, plus a tape recorder. Then, I thought of something more low-tech: a subscription to *National Geographic*. He loved the gift, in part because it met his language needs but more because his son began to enjoy reading as well. Encouraged, I gave a Xhosa colleague a user-friendly book on U.S. management, promising another each time I returned. Now, I never go without one in my bag. It is the repetition of this action that creates bonds. These items can also become status symbols, advertising the recipients' connection with you (and your firm) to their peers. By providing gifts that enhance their working image, you enhance yours.

Give a gift that can be resold. That idea violates the American belief that resale of gifts insults the giver. In Africa, however, giving gifts takes on new meaning. Gifts meant for resale can permit business counterparts to carry on their work in dignity. Consider, for instance, the story of a Western firm seeking licenses from a government department in the former Zaire. The responsible official demanded a cash bribe before granting the license. The Westerners countered by presenting gifts— in this case, home appliances. These were resold in the local black market and the resulting income not only led the African official to provide licenses but to also ask what else the firm might need. The Westerners duly made other requests and, of course, provided appropriate gifts in exchange for equally appropriate favors. Over time, key men on both sides became friends, as each side prospered. The same conditions exist in South Africa's townships. In zones where black marketing now supplements wage income, consider predeparture gifts in resale terms.

There are only three rules in this South African gift-giving game. One is to give first; it signals that you hope not just to do business but to become a friend. The next is to give often; generosity generates goodwill and therefore forges bonds. The final rule is to give selectively; you cannot have ties with everyone. Thus, restrict relationship building to key people, and provide gifts or services that label you as unique in their minds. Indeed, not only the gifts but all of your predeparture preparations should be managed so as to label you as unique in the minds of everyone you meet. Once you establish your concern for people (as well as products), you will be properly positioned to begin your venture.

References

Abrahams, Peter. 1971. *Wild Conquest*. New York: Anchor Books.

————. 1970. *Mine Boy*. New York: Collier Books.

Cadman, Anthony G. Chairman, Anthony Cadman Associates, South Africa. 1999. Personal conversations.

Dunn, Frederica Hoge. 1978. "The 'Best Man Theory' and Why It Fails." *New York Times* (16 July).

Economist. 1996. "Translate, The Beloved Country" (24 February).

Fitzpatrick, Percy. 1989. *Jock of the Bushveld*. Johannesburg: A. D. Donker.

Ignatieff, Michael. 1997. "Digging Up the Dead." *New Yorker* (10 November), 84–93.

Lanham, Peter, and A. S. Mopeli-Paulus. 1953. *Blanket Boy*. New York: Thomas Y. Crowell.

Mandela, Nelson. 1994. *Long Walk to Freedom*. London: Abacus Books, Little, Brown.

Michener, James A. 1980. *The Covenant*. New York: Random House.

Paton, Alan. 1953. *Too Late the Phalerope*. New York: Charles Scribner's Sons.

————. 1948. *Cry, the Beloved Country*. New York: Charles Scribner's Sons.

Petzinger, Thomas Jr. 1998. "The Front Lines." *Los Angeles Times* (2 April).

Roux, Edward. 1964. *Time Longer than Rope*. Madison, WI: University of Wisconsin Press.

Smiley, Xan. 1986. "A Black South Africa?" *Economist* (1 February), 34.

Sparks, Allister. 1996. *Tomorrow Is Another Country.* Chicago: University of Chicago Press.
Taylor, Stephen. 1994. *Shaka's Children: A History of the Zulu People.* London: HarperCollins, 216–35.

4

Getting Started:
Try African Business Methods

> There is a proper way to begin each thing. It is
> taught by our grandfathers' grandfathers. The
> dead must guide the living. The old must lead the
> young. Show me a place where the lambs teach
> the sheep and I will show you a nation of
> madmen.
>
> —Zulu elder

Seek African Allies (Not Sales)

There is a proper way, an African way, to begin a South African business venture. However, it is not the American way. We Americans are product oriented. Once abroad, we focus on presenting what we hope to sell. We are also fast paced and deadline oriented. We need to feel that we are making progress. That may mean establishing a business base immediately on landing (if needed, in hotel rooms), then racing to appointments, schedule in hand. At each stop, we extol the virtues of our product—which, after all, is why we have come. We seek "deals," which we usually define in terms of sales.

Having read this far, you now realize that most Africans are people oriented. On entering new business settings, they first search out key players, then learn the local rules. Thereafter, they look for increasingly influential contacts to teach them where and when to play. Only then do they display their product and enter the commercial game.

This people-centered option can be useful, especially if your firm has limited start-up funds. To learn the intricacies of this strategy, set product presentations to one side for your first weeks in this new setting, along with your time schedule and multistage marketing plan. Instead, devote this time to learning from local contacts, developing personal relationships, and then transforming the best of them into commercial allies.

You must realize, however, that the concept of alliance means something different in South Africa. The African worldview divides humanity into two groups: allies and competitors. Allies include those with whom one has relationships. Many Africans perceive themselves as living within an imaginary circle. Those inside the circle are related to each other, either by blood ties, marriage, or lifelong friendship. In fact, each circle forms an extended family, composed of both real and fictional kinsmen. In this worldview, all those with whom one has either real or fictional ties are classified as kinsmen and thus lifelong allies in a ceaseless struggle against competitors (enemies).

Competitors include all those outside one's family circle, thus all those with whom one has no relationship. They form competitive family circles, with each defining all the others as enemies, competing for available resources instead of sharing them. In economies of scarcity, this competition can be fierce. Most Africans view those with whom they lack ties as more than competitors; they are potential predators and not to be trusted. Consider a KhoiSan proverb:

> Can zebras know why lions hunt them?
> They cannot ask, so they run (and thus avoid them).

So it is with humans. Those with whom one has ties are harmless; one can share with them. All others may attack.

Africans feel most secure when encircled by kin from whom they can seek help. However, each competing circle can increase its security by seeking new recruits, whom they define as "brothers" and whom we might call allies. In Africa, however, alliance is defined in terms of kinship—real or fictional. If two men proclaim they are "brothers," address each other as "my brother," and behave thenceforth as kinsmen, who is to say they have not formed a fictional family, a brotherhood of comrades? Thereafter, if each is accepted (as a brother) into the other's family, the two circles will be linked, strengthening each. Thereafter, though their tie is fictional, they will behave as brothers should, each supporting the other throughout their lives.

In theory, this sense of brotherhood should permanently exclude you. In African eyes, you appear not only as an outsider but also as a potential predator. This simply means that you have neither real nor fictional ties. Common sense, then, suggests you launch your business venture by creating them. Since Africans seek allies as part of doing business, why not do the same?

Exploit Your Introductions

If you prepare before departure, you will arrive well armed with introductions provided by your contacts in the United States. Exploit them. Begin your South African assignment by interviewing each one. Take weeks to develop solid relationships with them; they hold the keys to commercial success. Make the first appointments during business hours, not to market your product but yourself. Use both your recent arrival and consequent inexperience as business tools, asking each new acquaintance what you should know, whom you should meet, and why. One British manager who does this outlines each stage of his project in every interview. Each time an African colleague suggests a problem, this manager does not ask how to solve it (as we might) but *who* might help him do so. Then he requests an introduction.

Your goal in these interviews is both to seek data and to develop two distinct types of contacts. One group should include useful members of the *formal* economic sector. They know the regulations and thus how things should be done. The second should include members of the *informal* (black market) economic sector. Ask them to teach you the alternatives. This second group can assume great importance in South Africa's informal economy, where few people follow regulations.

Your ultimate goal, however, is not only to seek allies among your peers but to move up the local social ladders so as to identify, meet, and eventually influence relevant decision makers. They may initially help only as a favor to the person who first contacted them on your behalf. However, they may then take an interest in you, both personally and as a representative of a U.S. firm. Consequently, helping you may offer them peer status, new U.S. contacts, and the chance that your project may fit their interests as well as yours.

Pivotal allies can provide critical help, particularly in the early stages of a project launch, where you feel least familiar with the rules. One influential contact can dissolve a bottleneck, while a second gets you preferential treatment. A highly placed official can become a mentor, guiding you through commercial and social minefields, where a misstep means disaster. In short, when entering regions where business works through relationships, common sense suggests you form them.

Shift to African Time

Relationships, of course, take time to build, particularly among those who share neither a common culture nor a common past. One useful way to start is to shift from U.S. to African time. Most Americans treat "African time" as a joke. We use the phrase as a synonym for being late. When Western friends ironically ask me if I will meet them "on African time," they are asking if I plan to be late. Their humor suggests there is only one system of time in the world—theirs! In fact, there are two.

One system might be called "scientific time," since it is based on Western science. It assumes most human activities should last for specified durations. Thus, executives in most U.S. companies plan meetings to last fifty minutes, with ten more for coffee. Most messages on answering machines take less than one minute to relate. If we are five minutes late for an appointment, we offer a one-sentence apology that is always accepted. If ten minutes late, we make a longer apology plus an explanation. After twenty minutes, those awaiting us grow angry. After thirty, they leave (Hall 1983).

This system operates in North America (excluding Mexico), northwestern Europe, nations settled by northwest Europeans (Australia, etc.), and among elites of other nations that have accepted Western concepts of time. Americans, however, expect to operate on scientific time across the world. We perceive time as limited, and therefore too precious to either waste or lose. We "kill" time by doing nothing. We use time to complete tasks. We prefer to make progress, rather than make friends (Hall).

Africans use a second system, which might be called "natural time," since it is based on natural levels of comfort in the human body. Originally, it was also based on seasonal rather than scientific observations. As a result, this system moves slowly, providing lower levels of stress to those who use it, as illustrated in a traditional Zulu proverb:

> *Umsebenzi hawuqedwa* (The work should
> never end).

It implies that tasks should be enjoyed, not hurried to completion. A more recent Xhosa proverb declares,

> God gave time to Africans but (only)
> watches to Europeans.

It equates natural with comfortable and scheduling with stress.

Americans may not realize that this second system is the most widespread on earth. It operates in much of Africa, Asia, the Middle East, Latin America, the Caribbean and Pacific Islands, as well as Russia, the Mediterranean, and Eastern Europe to a lesser degree. Its users also share a common philosophy. They perceive time as unlimited. It flows in cycles, so that missed opportunities will eventually recur. It operates on multiple levels, allowing people to work on several things at once. Its prime purpose is not to provide the frameworks to complete tasks (as in the West), but to develop and nurture the relationships with other people that provide the only true security. A Bantu proverb reflects this philosophy:

> Wealth is only meat. Chew and it is gone. It
> is the talk [that others bring to meals] which
> fills the stomach.

Time Conflicts

These systems are not complementary. Ours idealizes fixed time frames, punctuality, deadlines, and chronological precision. Theirs emphasizes physical comfort, social enjoyment, and personal relaxation. We therefore clash in contemporary business settings. One conflict concerns commercial punctuality. We equate it with commercial effectiveness and deride lateness as inefficiency (Levine 1985). Significant or frequent delays by supervisors, peers, or subordinates are perceived as expressions of contempt.

However, Africans have their own beliefs regarding punctuality. Consider this report on a recent conference of the National African Federated Chamber of Commerce/South Africa (NAFCOC) from the perspective of commercial punctuality:

> The proceedings were due to start at 9 A.M.
> However the first people only began to arrive at
> 9:45...although most of the hotels were within
> walking distance.... Some scheduled speakers
> did not turn up [at all] and no explanation was
> given for their absence. (Mkhuma 1996, 86)

Americans are likely to disapprove of such behavior; Africans might not. In fact, each incident reflects one aspect of an African philosophy regarding how time should be used. In Bantu culture, time is used to both display and magnify high status. The more important a person, the later he may be—since notables are not expected to be punctual. The NAFCOC audience was forty-five minutes late, thus reflecting the status they derived as conference attendees. The speakers came still later or not at all, reflecting their higher status. The audience received no explanation because none was needed. Delay and absence were and still are accepted as prerogatives of power. American attempts to override them can generate intense resentment. Indeed, many South African blacks regard our efforts to do this as

> an extension of the Apartheid system, which
> forced Africans to work within limited time
> frames as a punishment, and an enslavement to
> Black people who feel that work should be
> enjoyed. (Zama 1996)

We also clash with Africans over commercial deadlines. Americans often try to make them as early as possible—sometimes arbitrarily, since finished projects may then sit for days on supervisors' desks. We feel the shortest time frames provide subordinates with the greatest sense of urgency, thus improving both their productivity and enjoyment of the task. Since we constantly prioritize, the project with the shortest deadline looms largest in our minds. As a result, we maximize our professional efforts by imposing dual deadlines, externally on each other and internally on ourselves. We complain about our deadlines but actually enjoy meeting them. Too often, however, we assume that foreigners must feel the same. Many, of course, do not.

Africans react differently to deadlines. Many feel they interfere with solving problems. "Big Men" (notables) derive instant status from coping with big problems. The more time required to solve one, the greater it must be, and thus the greater their prestige. If you hurry them, requesting a solution in the minimum possible time, you diminish that prestige. Worse, by imposing a deadline, you imply lack of trust and thereby impugn their honor.

I learned this the hard way with an African carpentry team I had hired to work on my home. I asked how long the job would take. Not wanting to offend me but unwilling to limit themselves, they replied "not long." Since I was paying by the hour, I told them to finish it in three days. They put down their tools, left the site, complained to a local official, and then returned with that official and sixty chanting, delighted onlookers to demand my public apology. They received it—in their language. In South Africa, if a conflict arises between the American need for deadlines and the African sense of human dignity, it would seem wise to weigh both sides before you act.

Much of South Africa now runs on African time. Sometimes, African elitists, familiar with American business practice, will meet your expectations with regard to both arrival times and deadlines. Sometimes they will be as late as seems appropriate for both their social status and yours. In such cases, you may wish to adjust.

One useful option is to schedule meetings but expect to wait, and fill the time with paperwork from your briefcase. If your contact is late, he will apologize. If he fails to appear, a subordinate will send you home with apologies and a request to return. Once you see no insult is intended, you will have begun your adjustment to African time.

A second approach is to use African tradition. In the United States, if a man steals my car, sells it, and is then caught and jailed, I still may not retrieve my vehicle. In South Africa, if a man steals my cow, sells it, and is caught, he must return another cow of equal value as well as several goats to compensate my suffering. That analogy can appeal to African colleagues. By coming late or missing deadlines, I argue that they steal "sheep" (time) from me. By working late, they can return it—along with extra "goats" (minutes) to compensate my suffering. Often, perhaps amused by my appeal to their tradition, they agree.

A final method is to use African time to form African ties, to chat with others in the office. This has two advantages. First, it satisfies the American need for action (to do something), reducing the anxiety we feel when forced to wait (and do nothing). Second, each new contact expands your chances of creating an alliance, since he will discuss you, your firm, and your project with peers, debating both your value to their projects and whether you seem worthy of their trust. It will be useful, therefore, to transform "lost time" into "talking time," learning more about key individuals with whom you work.

Adjust to Ambiguity

One problem that will appear while conversing with African contacts is their fondness for linguistic ambiguity. We value linguistic precision, orally and in writing. In business, we prefer to be direct and brief. Our conversational goal is to get to the point. We expect machines to operate precisely and predictably. We train staff to perform in precise and predictable ways. We quantify even the most intangible data, for by doing so we feel able to predict the results.

Most Africans do not mind commercial imprecision. While individuals can operate precisely, certain communal traditions work against being specific. Verbal ambiguity, for instance, is seen as an art. As a result, business can be more artfully conducted by salting conversation with proverbs, with all sides taking pleasure in deciphering the hidden meanings. It is a mark of verbal elegance to work these sayings into conversations. Since they have greater impact then ordinary words, they are more often seen as true (Ahiauzu 1986). Consequently, African business discussion can flow at several levels, allowing participants to learn about potential colleagues as well as their proposals.

Africans also value numerical ambiguity. Traditionally, for people to state precisely what they owned—be it cattle, commercial goods, or contraband—was considered arrogant and impolite. Such declarations were also believed to anger the ancestral spirits of those involved, who would retaliate by sending illness into the community. In consequence, when you seek precise, numerical responses to commercial questions, modern African entrepreneurs, aware of how negatively Whites still react to the mention of ancestral spirits or proverbs in a business setting, may simply evade specificity. Christianity has eroded ancestral beliefs, but many still respect tradition.

Africans also equate verbal ambiguity with entertainment, even when doing business. Orators and storytellers command wide respect. Each orator has an area of expertise, each storyteller a beloved story. Each time a tale is retold, it can be embellished with linguistic flourishes and thereby evolve into verbal art. Bantu businessmen believe in these traditions and enjoy embellishing what we prefer to be direct discussion.

I once spoke, for instance, with a senior Zulu manager about a staffing crisis. He described the problem. I offered a brief, direct, American-style suggestion. He reworded my response, then diverged from the topic in a flow of oratory that drew him far away from staffing and back a hundred years in Zulu history. I wondered how he could move so far from his original problem—only to realize he was heading back to it. Ten minutes later, he had a solution (based on my idea) that suited us both. Timidly, I found the courage to ask why he had drifted so far off the topic. "Who drifted?" he replied. "Look back at what we learned on the way." On reflection, I saw that, although taking time for other topics, he had enjoyed orating and I had enjoyed listening. From those perspectives, our attempt to solve a business problem was a mutual success.

African tradition offers solid social reasons to justify this pride in ambiguity. It seems commercially imprudent to dismiss this strategy as less effective than our own. Since U.S. business methods do require solid data, why not inquire in African ways? A Bantu proverb is helpful here:

> Night, our mother, is the best adviser.

This implies that wisdom lies in taking problems home each evening to share with kin and comrades. Over many nights, you may hear many answers. Only after hearing a sufficient number can you choose.

This wisdom can apply in modern settings. When seeking commercial data, supply African counterparts with specifics to signal that you seek serious ties. Then, ask for correspondingly specific detail. If they respond in ambiguities, probe gently to see if you can win their trust. Thereafter, cross-check whatever data you receive with other sources. Keep asking. Specifics are often simply unavailable. Repeat your questioning until you can predict the answers, no matter whom you ask. Africans will use the same method of repeated inquiry with regard to you.

Visit and Play Host

A visit, like an interview, is a business tactic used to cultivate allies. Spend your business hours interviewing in the first few weeks, but visit or play host each evening. This shift may irritate you if you work both days and evenings, especially if you consider frequent and repeated visits nonproductive. However, African businessmen find endless time to visit, both at local drinking places and at each other's homes. These visits are where business actually begins; by socializing, they are laying the basis for acquaintance and thus alliance. Logic suggests you do the same.

That will require learning the three most relevant African visitation rules: *Visits are obligatory, visits are impulsive,* and *visits are unending.* Whether in cities, townships, or villages, tradition requires perpetual visiting. Everyone knows whom to visit, when, and why. Individual deviation leads to general condemnation. Modern influences have blurred these customs to a degree, but even Westernized Africans in urban settings know whom to visit and when to expect visitors.

The system works through its unending reciprocity. Each visit generates others, as former guests become hosts and hosts become guests. Custom requires everyone to visit; to be alone is to be accused of plotting witchcraft. In Bantu culture, to win trust you must relate to others—a rule that may also be applied to you.

If you are invited to the homes of African colleagues, you may expect to meet several local Big Men on each occasion, all drawn from the social and professional networks of the host. If you appear on time, you will be the first to arrive. The Africans will arrive according to local status, with the Big Men coming last. They will sit informally around the foreign guest and become acquainted, while less prestigious guests move to the circle's outer edge. The sharing of meat, conversation, laughter, and liquor is intended to create relationships among you all.

As the visit ends, however, each guest can incur communal obligations that have no U.S. parallels. One is to nurture the relationships you have just formed. As you may have pondered how each person can fit into your business plans, so have they done with you. Having accepted hospitality for just this purpose, each guest now feels obligated to provide it—not only to the host but to other significant members of his circle as well. Custom offers two ways to discharge this obligation. One is to play host in turn. The second is to welcome any member of that group who may impulsively drop by your home (or hotel) to strengthen the newly formed relationship with you.

If you are unaware of these unspoken expectations, you may both disappoint an African host and jeopardize a means of market entry. Americans have different visiting rules. We let two reciprocal invitations end a social cycle, rather than each invitation endlessly begetting others. We also restrict reciprocity to individuals and spouses instead of groups. We often transform our homes into castles, and we pull the drawbridge up except on prior invitation. Many of us neither visit on impulse nor welcome drop-in visitors. We may thus react ungraciously when Africans drop by on impulse, expecting to be welcomed. Therein lies the conflict. From their perspective, dropping by is a communal obligation; from ours, it can violate both our personal time and private space.

For these reasons, some adjustment to African visiting customs will often lead to unanticipated opportunities. There is no need to constantly have parties. If you do, however, it may prove useful to invite all the significant guests you meet at prior functions, not just the hosts. It may also be worthwhile to encourage drop-in visits, thus transforming your home from a moated castle to an open courtyard, where local notables feel welcome to come by. Such adjustments will be well received in African business circles as signaling a wish to do business their way.

Do Favors: Create Dependence

Africans give and accept favors to enlist allies. In business, this takes the form of deliberately providing both personal and commercial services, intended explicitly to place receivers under obligation and thereby generate new relationships. The cycle begins when one person does something for another but asks nothing in return. The recipient then feels obligated to eventually return the favor and will do so when asked. This initial exchange serves as social glue. Instead of ending the cycle by uttering the magic incantation "Thank you" (as we do), his reciprocal favor reobligates the original provider. He must reciprocate in turn, thereby perpetuating a cycle that may last throughout their lives. Consider this example:

> When our house burned down…nine years ago,
> our neighbors collected…$13,000…along with
> old clothes, dishes, pots, pans [and then] found
> us the house where we now live.… As other
> villagers have hit trouble, we have slowly been
> repaying their bounty. (Sayle 1998, 84)

One way to launch this cycle is to sense another person's needs without inquiring, then meet them—perhaps superficially at first, but more thoroughly on closer acquaintance. Another is to work to attain what Americans might call "Godfather" status (and South Africans, "Big Man" status), a social and economic position of such eminence as to permit you to meet requests for favors as they occur, thereby gradually surrounding yourself with dependent clientele. Both methods place receivers under obligation. African commerce functions through the perpetual provision and repayment of such favors, making them a useful business tool. The alliances that emerge through constant giving and receiving are far stronger than can result from either money payments or written contracts.

Assume, for instance, that your firm seeks licenses from a government department headed by a Sotho. If you pay another Sotho a fee to help procure them, your firm incurs no further obligation; your payment ends the relationship. If the Sotho works without a fee, however, he performs a favor. Your firm therefore owes him a favor, to be granted at his request. If he subsequently provides additional favors, your sense of obligation should intensify. If you return the favors (or anticipate his needs and then provide them), he becomes increasingly obligated in turn.

Since both sides benefit from this emerging alliance, the exchange may continue—irregularly, but indefinitely. Over time, the feelings generated by these exchanges should allow your relationship to evolve from one of acquaintances to colleagues, to friends, and finally (from a Bantu perspective) into fictional kinship. The system works. Failure to repay a favor can trigger internal shame, social condemnation, and the fear of ancestral disapproval. To those who learned these things as children, such beliefs are very real.

The Elder Brother Strategy

Favors can also be exchanged between people of unequal status. Wealthy Bantu businessmen follow what we might call an "Elder Brother Strategy," seeking both communal and commercial status through recurrent acts of generosity to subordinates. Their goal is to place recipients under permanent obligation. In so doing, they assume the role of elder brothers to those they help. Those receiving favors take on the role of younger brothers. Unable to repay the favors they receive in equal measure, younger brothers pay symbolically by providing token gifts and acts of deference, while placing time and energy at the elder brother's disposal.

This strategy can please both sides. I am elder brother to several Africans. Our relationships began when I initially provided advice regarding education, finding work, and dealing with government agencies. I act on any favor they request within my expertise. They respond with gifts, deference, hospitality, and action on any favor I request within their means or expertise. Obviously, they prove invaluable when I visit their homelands, as I prove invaluable when they enter mine.

The Elder Brother concept is not, of course, unique to South Africa. The Japanese call it *nawabushi* (to make someone owe you favors). Filipinos speak of *utang na loob* (inner debt) to describe a cycle in which everyone owes and is owed favors. Congolese use a proverb to describe a similar cycle that continues beyond death, since the obligations of fathers pass to sons.

Money cannot bury you; only kinfolk can.

We Americans rarely use this kind of relationship. In South Africa, we should.

Let me introduce a commercial example: the Elder Brother Strategy developed by Kellogg Corporation, South Africa, Ltd., to market breakfast cereal. Having saturated the small European market by 1985, it wished to penetrate the far larger African market. Although the nation was still under apartheid, Kellogg's problem was not racial segregation but Bantu custom. Africans eat cornmeal porridge for breakfast, if they breakfast at all. To penetrate this market, the firm had to convince clients to violate centuries of tradition.

Kellogg started small, hoping to transform its image from white outsider to elder brother. The first step was to employ Africans. Thereafter, it moved outside the workplace into its workers' homes, subsidizing their mortgages and new construction. Next, it reached out to their children, providing teacher training for their schools (Hoerr 1986).

The schools then became the channel through which tradition could be changed. Kellogg's advertising ties consumption of its product to maintaining health through a balanced diet—a topic easily introduced into class instruction and aimed precisely at those age groups most receptive to new ideas. In consequence, by placing both the students and their parents in its debt, Kellogg's corporate image evolved from outsider to employer, to teacher and, ultimately, to elder brother. Since lessons taught in these schools can also be passed on to others, the firm has found both a channel through which to disseminate its message and the image required to make it acceptable.

The Younger Brother Strategy

The counterpart to the Elder Brother Strategy is the "Younger Brother Strategy." This strategy works particularly well for Africans launching first-time business ventures and takes the form of accepting both personal and business favors from related individuals (ideally, older kinsmen) with greater wealth and influence. The response to this assistance is to assume a dependent (younger brother) role, providing symbolic favors, deference, and service. Unlike Americans, Africans find dependence both desirable and dignified. By depending on fathers, they argue, sons honor them. By depending on teachers, students learn and honor their teachers. By depending on established sponsors, entrepreneurs have a chance to get a foothold.

Africans assume this role for other reasons as well. South Africa's legal framework offers consumers virtually no protection. They do business in a climate of uncertainty. The lack of quality control, product guarantees, and physical security creates anxiety. Emerging entrepreneurs may therefore seek the security provided by an elder brother, assuming the younger brother role in exchange for membership (however fictional) in an influential extended family.

Americans may also find this option useful, particularly when first establishing their business presence in what still may seem a very foreign setting. One African American I met in Swaziland has utilized the Younger Brother Strategy since he arrived. He first came as a tourist, then saw a business opportunity in the work of Swazi artists. He initially bought products for resale in America but later realized that his major market might well be the foreign tourists in Swaziland itself.

His next step was to develop close relationships with members of a notable Swazi clan. Through them he gained the additional connections, influence, and sponsorship required to establish an artists' collective. Having prospered, he responded to those who first extended favors by providing a service that places them clearly in his debt: he pays their children's school fees. He remains a younger brother in their extended family and has used that strategy to gain both economic security and social respect.

Get Wired

Rethink your start-up options in the context of an electrical analogy. You will enter a zone within which individuals cluster in mutually competing groups. Innumerable (although imaginary) wired circuits connect the individuals within each group, while occasional wires also run between clusters. Each of your African contacts holds a mental finger on an imaginary switch. Should he push it, vocal electricity will flow toward selected allies, who will take action in response to his requests. He can be switched on in turn by any member of his system seeking favors from him.

This system must compete, however, against its neighbors. All members must therefore stay wired in, maintaining what may be hundreds of connections by visits, gifts, and favors. Moreover, members must ceaselessly recruit influential individuals from other groups, including influential foreigners, thus strengthening their own group.

As a new arrival with no connections of your own, you have two options. One is to ignore these systems altogether, focusing solely on the effective presentation of your product and remaining, permanently, on the periphery of African commercial interaction. The other is to analyze competing systems and "wire in" to those most relevant to your specific venture. Follow three simple rules:

1. Give selectively
2. Give first
3. Keep giving

You will discover that generosity can generate allies. In short, one way to tap African markets is to try African methods.

References

Ahiauzu, Augustine. 1986. "The African Thought System and the Work Behavior of the African Industrial Man." *International Studies of Man and Organizations* 16, no. 2: 37–58.

Hall, Edward T. 1983. *The Dance of Life*. New York: Anchor/Doubleday, 44–58.

Hoerr, John. 1986. "Kellogg's Private War against Apartheid." *Business Week* (23 September), 107.

Levine, Robert. 1985. "It Wasn't the Time of My Life." *Discover* (December), 66–71.

Mkhuma, Zingisa. 1996. "NAFCOC Conference Under Fire." *Enterprise* (November); a magazine for black Republic of South Africa entrepreneurs.

Sayle, Murray. 1998. "The Social Contradictions of Japanese Capitalism." *Atlantic Monthly* (2 June).

Zama, Reginald. (1996). Unofficial *nduna* (spokesman) for thirty University of Zululand students who provided oral and written commentary on issues dealt with in this chapter.

5

How to Work
with an African Firm

> Company director Albert Koopman yanked off
> his tie and jacket, sprawled on to the ground and
> invited the black labor activist to step on him.
> "You get one chance! After that, you must stop
> blaming me for the sins of 300 years of white
> South Africans. After that, you must try to allow
> us to work together!"
>
> —Ned Temko

Large South African companies are owned either by white
South Africans or by foreigners. A few others are now partially or wholly headed by members of the African political
elite. These run along Western lines. However, many small and
midsized enterprises are African owned, having appeared across
the country since The Turn in 1994. These are run the African
way, and they may share several traits with your firm: enthusiasm, inexperience, limited capital, and need for advice. Like
you, they may be commercial upstarts, pioneering in new fields.
One or more may prove useful as a sponsor, formal partner, or
informal ally. The analysis in this chapter assumes you will
wish to work with at least one of them, exchanging relevant
expertise.

Such a decision, however, can lead to unexpected conflicts,
for these companies are often organized and managed in ways
that are unfamiliar to Americans. I learned this by asking a

Western-educated African businessman exactly how his firm was structured. He said it had no structure. I asked why he told me something we both knew was nonsense. His reply: "I do not feel you Whites can grasp the facts. Our firms are not structured in ways you understand. You Americans ignore our methods in any case. Why not provide the answer you expect?"

Respect African Management Methods

This man is right. We ignore African management methods, both in American business schools and in corporate training programs. As a result, few U.S. managers know these methods exist, and fewer still actually analyze them in order to adjust their own American procedures before launching African ventures. Instead, most equate African concepts with a primitive past. "There is a racist overlay to it...the dark continent thing, the Tarzan imagery. Americans can't imagine there are highly competent, potential African partners out there" (Strugatch 1992).

Americans often deliberately restrict their dealings to the Westernized firms, which they assume use Western methods. This approach flies in the face of history. I suggested earlier that African commercial methods have been refined by the continent's great trading tribes for over two thousand years. In that time, they have achieved degrees of managerial complexity and marketing effectiveness that we would do well to analyze and learn from.

Nor are the continent's contemporary trading companies either primitive or small. Many operate across national borders. I know one extended family of so-called street peddlers that imports animal carvings from Hong Kong through central Kenya to downtown Durban. One group of clans creates and then exports fake antique masks from Africa through Paris to New York (Lemann 1987). In Johannesburg, extended families have formed syndicates that carjack BMWs for transfer to Zaire in exchange for stolen gold (Schissel 1989; McEvoy

1996). Their methods, shaped by African tradition, work too well within contemporary commerce for us to ignore.

Every South African firm is unique, reflecting the peculiarities of its regional, tribal, and family origins. That notwithstanding, most Bantu businessmen organize, finance, manage, and market their commercial concepts in surprisingly similar ways. These ancestral ideals remain intact in the minds of even the most Westernized entrepreneur. This is particularly true of the current generation of business leaders, now in their forties or older. Most of them grew up in tradition-oriented rural settings, where they absorbed beliefs to which they still adhere. In adulthood, these concepts stay very much alive within their minds, offering time-honored alternatives to Western business practices. It can be useful to recognize and acknowledge the power of these ancient business principles and to modify your own approach in dealing with them.

External Image: The Chameleon Strategy

You may initially wish, for example, to adjust your perception of the external image that certain African firms project. Often it will seem so Westernized that you will assume you can work with the firm in Western ways. This may prove unexpectedly difficult. My African colleagues often describe their firms as having "black hearts and white skins," meaning they present a Westernized external image while retaining an entirely African core. This management concept, based on the chameleon's capability to change color and blend in, has developed from centuries of white exploitation that forced Blacks to outwardly display Western behaviors while inwardly preserving indigenous beliefs.

Sometimes both styles function simultaneously, as when Africans organize their offices along European lines, with desks set up in tidy rows, while supervisors work behind closed doors. In fact, both managers and staff may ignore the physical layout to spend their time in clusters, mixing conversation with commercial progress.

When first visiting this type of firm, therefore, one goal will be to look beneath its skin. You may be met by Western-educated counterparts with Western business titles in Western-furnished offices. They may offer Western-style refreshments, while a Western-trained secretary records your discussions in English. Nonetheless, you will not be dealing with a Western firm. Behind the scenes, decisions made at the heart of the company will be African. To influence those decisions, you must move beyond the reception rooms and probe into the structure of the firm itself.

Internal Structure: Firm Equals Family

One place to begin this investigation is by forming ties with the designated spokesman the firm assigns to deal with you. He may be English speaking, Western trained, and commercially expert, yet lack decision-making power in the organization. This may be because most African companies are structured differently from ours. American firms are often structured like the U.S. Army, with one chief commanding a vertical hierarchy based on clear chains of command. We hire and promote staff on merit. We define superior/subordinate relations by written contract, and informally restrict relations between them to business. We specialize, assigning each person to specific tasks. We follow rules.

In contrast, Africans organize their companies like extended families. The founder, an elder, is placed at the center of several imaginary circles, composed of near and then more distant kin. The inner circle will consist of "age-mates" (men of his generation), who share a body of knowledge based on decades of shared experiences. Since they collectively direct the enterprise, we might call them a CEO and board of directors. Nonetheless, unlike American executives and board members, they may all be kin.

A second circle may hold men of middle age, the sons and sons-in-law of the founding generation. Through foreign schooling, members of this group may acquire special skills—commercial, linguistic, or even military. They would therefore either work as specialists (e.g., interpreting, marketing) or supervise departments composed of younger kin. They are not promoted for merit but remain subordinate to every elder throughout their lives.

Over time, outer circles develop, perhaps less neatly organized than those preceding them. One circle would certainly hold adult grandchildren of the founding generation. Others might contain more distant relatives, their friends, and friends of friends. All may perceive themselves as members of the extended family. The further from the core, the more fictional the kinship becomes, with those of lowest status simply acting out the kinsman role by identifying with the family and firm.

This system permits no distinctions between family and business interests. Supervisors and subordinates are not linked by contract but by family ties. It is thus impossible to restrict relationships to business. If your supervisor is also your uncle, commercial and personal concerns will overlap. Nor are staff restricted to specific tasks. "Like any family," one man assured me, "if a thing needs doing, one of us does it." Promotion is also less relevant in family settings; no nephew can move up past an uncle. Nonetheless, the fact that the business *is* a family can lead to levels of business informality (as well as a disregard of formal rules) that you may find disconcerting and might mislabel as corruption.

To know you are dealing with a family can be useful, particularly when first evaluating its spokesman. Look beyond his commercial title, linguistic skills, and business qualifications to consider his age. If young or middle-aged, he may be a figurehead, chosen to deal with you because of his Western business training and English skills. The real decisions will come from the company's elders.

The next step is to ask to whom within the firm this spokesman is related and how. The need to ask this question may surprise you, since it has no parallel in U.S. business practice.

The sheer number of his in-house family ties may surprise you as well. Take notes as he describes the complex web of relationships. Learning the intricacies of kinship in this type of firm means acquiring a flow chart of its structure. If your spokesman is well connected, take advantage of his English to both explain your project and involve him in it. Make him an ally. Then ask him to introduce you to those kinsmen who make the actual decisions.

In-House Authority: Rank Equals Age

You may have two further adjustments to make when trying to influence the decision makers in this type of firm: exploiting your age and theirs. Age is a primary tool of African management. American firms confer authority according to competence and achievement, whether derived from experience, training, or brilliance. African authority flows from old to young, and no exceptions are made for commercial expertise. This springs from a belief equating longer years of life with more experience and therefore greater wisdom. Africans believe that aging "cools" the blood, allowing elders to consider problems more carefully. Even in firms that seem outwardly Westernized, the "hot-blooded" young are said to create conflicts, while the elderly use their wisdom to cool them.

The wisdom attributed to aging is also based on the African belief in the commercial value of both intuition and emotion. We feel these traits interfere with business and thus try to ignore or suppress them so as to decide issues rationally. The elders themselves contend that the wisdom gained through their years of experience is best expressed in terms of how they feel, emotionally and intuitively, both about specific proposals and about those proposing them. Such feelings need not be based on Western-generated commercial expertise. Rather, they emerge through consultation and quiet meditation, as their life experiences guide each new decision.

One commercial manifestation of this philosophy is that

supervisors must be older than subordinates. In massive operations like the Rand Gold Mines, where thousands of men from dozens of tribes must work together, spokesmen from every language group sort out who is older and should get preference in the work. Among Africans, matching rank and age is more than an organizing principle; it is tradition.

There are at least three ways to apply the age factor when opening discussions with this type of firm. One is to exploit your age. Your actual age may be less important than how you look. In the United States, we strive to look younger; in South Africa, you should strive to look older. I have brown hair and a white beard. In the United States I shave the latter; spokesmen for the Silicon Valley firms I deal with value a high-energy, relatively youthful image. In South Africa, I let my beard grow; my African contacts value my age and feel I have developed wisdom.

The age factor is also relevant when selecting additional Americans for South African assignment and again when hiring African staff. Choose older employees of either sex. Gender need be no barrier to commercial respect in South Africa. An older American woman, married and with children, may be perceived as wise. Just remember, the younger your firm's representative (male or female), the more likely that he or she will not be viewed as a spokesperson and thus will be shut out of the decision making.

Finally, reshape the thrust of your written proposals to appeal to the elders. American "action plans" sound better to young executives than to those with decades of experience. Most older people prefer gradualism. Once you learn that elders make the final decisions, present an approach that seems sufficiently unhurried to engage them.

Decision Making: Exploit African Time

The most difficult problem you may face in dealing with any African firm is obtaining a swift and timely decision. Remember that African decision making is based on "natural time." It is grounded in three uniquely African management tools: timelessness, consultation, and consensus. Unfortunately, all three clash with American managerial expectations. We prefer fixed deadlines and individual decisions; we reject consensus building as too slow. We also strive for speed (which we call "timeliness") and admire swift decisions, praising those who "wing it" or "think on their feet."

Africans prefer decisions to be reached through consultation and consensus, without reference to fixed times. Although African managers can make snap judgments as rapidly as anyone else, they remain aware of ancestral obligations regarding the need for consultation. By acting alone they flout their group's collective wisdom; by consulting, they honor it. Most Africans simply find their relaxed pace more satisfying than the American time-efficient approach.

Unfortunately, most Americans do not know what actually occurs in consensual decision making and grow unduly anxious when working with Africans who use it. To alleviate this anxiety, break the consultation into stages, learn what occurs in each stage, and actively join in so that you can influence the results.

Assume, for instance, that you seek a decision from a Zulu extended-family firm regarding long-range cooperation in the first joint retailing project to be established in its township. The Zulu call the consensus-building process *Ndaba*. To Ndaba is to assemble, consult, and thereby build consensus. An Ndaba is a gathering of elders, one representing each branch of an extended family (plus other allied families), to collectively decide a course of action.

The initial stage of an Ndaba is simply one of social and commercial introductions. You should be introduced by someone older who is already linked to elders in the company. By making the introduction, he sponsors you, thereby signaling his belief in your sincerity. By providing appropriate gifts and following proper ritual, you signal a belief in theirs.

The second stage will focus on allowing the recipients of your proposal to learn more about you as the proposer. On presenting a proposal, most Americans expect a swift reply. However, Africans spend this stage in consultation with the outsider, to evaluate both his business concept and himself. This may mean hours (or days) of back-and-forth visiting and considerable drinking. As we idealize efficiency and speed, they idealize unhurried deliberation.

In time, the company's elders gather for the next stage of Ndaba, which we might label "in-house consultation." Acting as an informal board of directors, older men will consult with relevant department heads. They will also consult outside the firm, seeking additional opinions, most often from knowledgeable kinfolk and age-mates. If the proposal and its potential are important, discussions may spread across the township as more distant informants are drawn in. It will last, according to one senior African manager, until "every voice has spoken."

Only after every aspect of the issues you have raised has been examined does the final, decision-making stage begin, as specific options gradually emerge. Differences between opposing groups are resolved by bartering both related and nonrelated items in much the same manner as U.S. senators horse-trade current votes for future favors to create legislation.

Final decisions are based on four Bantu traditions. First, consensus must emerge through discussion; spoken words have mystic power, and speaking together allows collective wisdom to emerge. Nothing need be written. Next, decisions must "feel" right to those concerned. As we believe in rational decisions, they extol the intuitive ability to sense appropriate actions. Agreement must also be collective; no one elder can gain so much wisdom as to direct a group. Only if everyone assents can harmony prevail. Finally, all decisions must be tentative. Often, accord is only reached on general principles, with details to be settled later. As a result, every decision is subject to change.

Africans feel this method of decision making has commercial value. Ignoring deadlines eliminates the need for haste. This in turn limits the possibility of future in-house conflict, since no minority would oppose a consensus so carefully constructed. This measured pace maintains harmony among participants, which facilitates the subsequent implementation.

Your inability to predict just when specific decisions will be made may generate anxiety. You can, however, work to influence those judgments you cannot hasten. Use African time in African ways. Begin with what Americans would normally perceive as an unwarranted delay by growing acquainted with each significant decision maker. Then, check out the firm's reputation among competing clans.

To increase your effectiveness (if costs permit), bring as many other U.S. staff on scene as you need to create an on-site research team. Insert them into the Ndaba by introducing each one to the firm's decision makers. Then instruct your team members to join the decision making by actively influencing key personnel at every level of the enterprise. This is, after all, what a group of African outsiders would do, were they in your place. It is by joining the decision-making process that you facilitate decisions.

Cofund Joint Ventures

One problem that can arise after agreements have been made concerns how an emerging alliance should be funded. This can derive from stereotypes held by both sides. Many African firms seek alliances with Americans primarily to acquire capital. In exchange, they expect to contribute other assets, which may range from land and labor to local expertise. They may not expect to contribute capital of their own. Many American firms seek African partners primarily to acquire local knowledge. Nonetheless, when asked to provide *all* start-up funds for an allegedly joint venture, Americans may draw back, deciding their potential partners are capital deficient regardless of what else they offer. This is usually untrue. African companies often have access to capital.

Kinship Funding

If black entrepreneurs lack land, collateral, or influential connections, Western banks routinely ignore them. Even African-owned banks use European lending criteria when considering loans. In consequence, small and midsized African firms turn away from Eurocentric sources of financing to the older and more African concept of kinship funding. Traditional funding methods offer two options to someone seeking start-up capital. One is to seek loans from kin. The loan process has surprising similarities to our own. For example, a Zulu entrepreneur might proceed as follows:

- *Loan request.* This would initially be made to an older kinsman, who then serves as the applicant's sponsor, transmitting the request along extended-family and clan channels to more distant kin.

- *Credit check.* Elders gather in Ndaba to evaluate both the proposal and the proposer. In fact, they run the oral equivalent of a credit check, analyzing the financial behavior, drinking habits, sexual fidelity, respect for tradition, and community reputation of the proposer.

- *Loan approval.* If the request is granted, every clan family contributes a portion of the required funds, based on group perceptions of their social and economic standing. The rich contribute substantially; the poor, a symbolic amount. Contributors are thus motivated by both peer pressure and the wish to respond as tradition requires. Since clans may have hundreds of members, substantial sums can be raised.

- *Loan repayment.* The funds collected are described as "loans." In fact, no repayment is expected, nor would a written contract stating repayment terms even be considered. The loan is treated as a favor to the applicant. He thus incurs an obligation to return comparable favors to every donor, when requested.

Rotation Funding

The second method of obtaining capital looks beyond extended family to fictional kinsmen and friends. A Bantu proverb declares:

One finger cannot wash a face.

Nor can one family—even an extended family—easily finance a firm. Many African businessmen therefore seek capital through rotation funding.

The concept of rotation funding appears across Africa. In Republic of Congo, it is called *likelemba;* in Cameroon, *tontines*; in Togo, *ristourno*. Even in New Orleans, descendants of slaves once known as "Kongos" and "Guineas" form "marry and bury societies," hardly realizing they are based on traditional African practice. Black South Africans call rotation funds *gooi-gooi* (throwings), *umgalelo* (pourings), *mahodisana* (growings), and, most often, *stokvels* (men who pool money to buy livestock) (Thomas 1991).

These grassroots funds have become formidable rivals to Western-sponsored banks. By providing microloans to tens of thousands of African clientele, they collectively handle more money than the Western banking systems (Schissel). The most reputable groups operate according to four principles, each of which provides insight into their financial reliability.

1. *Members are kin.* Most stokvels restrict membership to those with close enough links (kinship, friendship, etc.) to know and trust one another in financial matters. Over time, shared financial interests act to deepen the bonds among members. Consequently, both social pressure and personal shame assure repayments. Inquiries into the nature and duration of a group's relationships can thus provide an initial indicator of reliability. The closer the relationships, the more secure the loan.

2. *Operations are public.* Unlike extended-family funding, stokvel members publicly shepherd the movement of funds.

Usually, the fund leader invites members to a monthly feast, providing food and beer. He gathers money from those attending, then instantly disburses it to *one* of the contributors, thereby allaying fears the funds will be stolen.

3. *Funds rotate.* If twelve women join a stokvel to meet, feast, drink, and contribute R200 per month, the group gains R2400 each meeting, which it then distributes to one of the twelve. Thus, each woman receives R2400 once yearly—enough to start or expand an enterprise. Beyond the capital, she gains contacts, advice, and assistance from the other members, all of whom wish her commercial success, thereby ensuring further donations.

4. *Either sex can control.* Men or women can form stokvels, assemble, and disperse funds. Both sexes can also work together in one association. However, female stokvels are believed most reliable, since women work primarily to educate their children, while men often spend earnings on themselves. Your inquiry into the many roles of women within a stokvel can thus provide another indicator of stability.

Both kinship funding and rotation funding are primary African methods that ensure that even small and midsized firms have access to capital. Be wary, therefore, if potential allies suggest that you alone provide funding for mutual ventures. African businesspeople, like businesspeople everywhere, will act most responsibly where funds (in appropriate percentages) are invested by both sides.

Enlisting Allies: Seek Homeboy Status

The ultimate problem, once other questions are settled, is how to transform your personal image from American outsider to working partner and friend. Use the African homeboy strategy. Remember that Africans expand their business interests by seeking allies beyond their own extended families. To do this, they build relationships with "homeboys."

In South Africa, a homeboy (homegirl) is someone with whom you share aspects of a common past and, therefore, common values. Homeboys across Africa base this relationship on common geographic, linguistic, tribal, or clan roots. Homeboy status can instantly link two strangers in a foreign land the moment both realize they share a language, dialect, home village, clan, or tribe. They react by regarding one another as brothers and assuming the obligations of kin. I watched this occur between two Uganda Batusi, who met coincidentally in KwaZulu. Having initially identified each other by appearance (Batusi are strikingly slender and tall) and then by regional dialect, they formally addressed one another as "brother" and behaved thereafter as family.

Homeboy status can also emerge between two strangers who discover they share just one aspect of a common past. Often this is expressed in proverbs. Those who find they have had a common childhood ("We have shared the same dish"), have experienced the rite of circumcision ("We have shared the same knife"), or have had similar schooling or military service may form this type of brotherhood. Their common past provides shared values, and consequently a basis for relationship. In African terms, they become fictional kin.

Homeboys, like kinsmen, provide each other with favors and take on family obligations. They represent extensions of a firm's commercial reach, and therefore increase its economic security. A Tswana project manager in search of venture capital, for example, would turn first to close kinsmen, then distant ones, and finally go beyond extended-family circles to seek existing (or potential) homeboys. In this way, requests for aid expand outward like ripples in a pond, until favors are granted and solutions found.

In business, homeboys move easily between the roles of elder and younger brother, exchanging goods, services, and opportunities as circumstances and relationships demand. The system requires constant personal contact. African entrepreneurs strive to become personally engaged with each supplier, distributor, client, official, policeman, health inspector, border guard, smuggler, and anyone else who might legally or illegally influence their firms. They feel able to influence these people only when they become family. The head of one KwaZulu firm expressed this most clearly: "My employees are more than men who work for me. They are my friends. They are more than my friends. They are my sons. How else could I control them?"

The Rules/Exceptions Strategy

Homeboys, like kinsmen, are recruited by exchanging favors in such fashion as to create obligations. The type of favor most used in business, however, is to make exceptions to existing rules. I have mentioned earlier that Americans appreciate rules. When entering new business settings, especially in foreign nations, we ask what the rules are, then try to obey them. Where none exist, we often privately create them, feeling they add predictability to our lives. More important, we avoid exceptions to those rules. We may disagree with particular ones but still believe in them per se.

Africans, however, do business by making exceptions. They apply existing rules when needed but make exceptions for anyone related to them, including homeboys. This rules/exceptions strategy is quite deliberate; officials or others making the exceptions obligate recipients, thus creating or strengthening relationships. Consider this example: A Bantu manager learned that a homeboy had stolen funds from his white-owned firm. There was no way to conceal the theft, and Western law called for legal action. As a result, the European owner was not informed. Rather (since the stolen funds were spent), the manager solicited the same amount from other staff members having homeboy relationships with the thief. Repayment was made covertly; the thief remained free (Seddon 1989).

Here, the homeboy relationship between manager, thief, and employees was more important than either company regulations or national law, and an exception was made. The manager gained prestige by making it. The workers gained prestige by supporting the manager, helping a "brother" evade prison, and placing him in their debt. Although the thief had spent the stolen funds, he could gradually repay the borrowed sums in future favors. In this case, making an exception for one homeboy intensified the sense of brotherhood for everyone involved.

Can you seek homeboy status? Both the African need for personal involvement and their wish to draw useful individuals into extended families provide you with two tools with which to transform your outsider image. Why not use both to become homeboys? While it is true that African homeboys share portions of a common past, that need not shut us out. One U.S. former Peace Corps teacher is currently a homegirl to no fewer than ninety Gambians. She has remained within their memories for years. Would they hesitate to repay the favor she did them by providing education? Never.

I once surveyed the English-speaking members of a KwaZulu firm, seeking possible overlaps with my own past. One man was a Rotarian. Another had trained at Texas Tech. A third had interned in a U.S. bank. Another had taken religious instruction from American Baptists. Most Americans can find something in common with men like these. You need only explore their past and describe your own to discover what you share. Conversely, if you lack a common past, create a common present by spending time with members of their firm.

Americans often fail to put in the time required to win the respect of those with whom they work. Remember, one South African complaint is that we always draw away as the work day ends to socialize among our compatriots (Daley 1998). Why not reverse this pattern and behave like family, approaching African business colleagues from an African perspective? That means sharing not only gifts and favors but something of ourselves. Only by approaching Africans as equals, rather than as their advisers, can we expect them to involve themselves with us. Perhaps this attitude can be expressed most clearly by one final Bantu proverb:

> Your son is my son. Your friend is my friend.
> Your cares are my cares. Are we not brothers?

References

Daley, Suzanne. 1998. "For Black Americans in Black South Africa—A Chilly Reception." *San Francisco Chronicle* (8 April), A13.

Lemann, N. 1987. "Fake Masks." *New Yorker Magazine* (November), 24–37.

McEvoy, Chris. 1996. "South Africa's Most Stealable Cars." *You* (7 September), 14–15, and many similar articles in the Republic of South Africa press.

Schissel, Howard. 1989. "Africa's Underground Economy." *Africa Report* (January-February): 43–46.

Seddon, John. 1989. "The Development and Indignation of Third World Business: African Values in the Work Place." *Current Research in Management*, edited by V. Hamond, 43–46. London and Dover: Francis Pinter.

Strugatch, Warren. 1992. "Africa Does the East European Thing." *World Trade* (October): 78–83.

Temko, Ned. 1984. "S. Africa Firm Finds Black-White Power-Sharing Pays." *Christian Science Monitor* (July).

Thomas, Elmar. 1991. "Rotating Credit Associations." In *South Africa's Informal Economy*, edited by E. Preston-Whyte and C. Rogerson, 290–91. Cape Town: Oxford University Press.

6

On-Site Research

There is little evidence that marketing research is...used to any extent in underdeveloped countries.

—Harper Boyd, et al.

Marketers need to take cognizance that it is in the townships that trends develop. It is only by spending time in the townships...that relevant observations can be made.... Successful companies take time out to do research.... We can no longer wander blindly along hoping that everything will just fall into place.... All the more reason to employ qualified black [marketing and research] personnel.

—Robin Morris

Ignoring On-Site Research

As your relationships develop and you establish ties with other firms, you may decide to analyze your first potential market sites by employing, training, and then leading an African research team.

In theory, Americans approve of on-site research overseas. In practice we often skip it, particularly in third-world settings. Too often, our firms rely entirely on secondary data, collected safely in the United States. One study suggests that 75 percent of the first wave of American enterprises to enter China conducted no marketing research whatsoever. Some consulted secondary U.S. sources, but virtually none conducted on-site analysis in China itself (Lepage 1989). A similar study of U.S. firms in Brazil found that 50 percent did no on-site research, while 33 percent consulted U.S. documents exclusively. Only a few firms actually spoke with Brazilians (Erikson 1986). One Central African economist told me that no U.S. firm had *ever* conducted research in his country.

Nor do South African firms always research at home. One white enterprise, hoping to create a market among Zulus for Indian curry powder, repackaged the product with African themes (spears, shields, etc.), assuming it would draw black clientele. Had its officers conducted on-site research, they would have learned that Zulus (like Whites) equate curry with Indians, not Africans. "Zulu curry" was thus perceived as second-rate—and failed. Similarly, a soft drink company advertised its product with the slogan: "It's fun to be thirsty." Many South African Whites have never been truly thirsty. Many Blacks equate thirst with drought, which is not fun. Again, for lack of on-site research into what potential clients thought, the product failed (Morris 1992).

On-site research does pose problems in South Africa, where unpredictable events clash with our desire for predictable results. Many established American research methods fare badly among African clientele, whether rural or urban.

Response to written surveys, for example, can be so unpredictable as to range from low to none. There are reasons for this. Underpaid postmen have been known to dump bulk mail if the loads are too heavy. Rural recipients may ignore questionnaires, believing the written word less relevant than spoken interaction. Urban and township recipients may fear the written forms as unwarranted attention from vaguely envisioned "authorities"—whom they perceive as uniformly malevolent. Female heads of households may simply hesitate to answer strangers. Men sometimes post the forms on walls as symbols of prestige. What Americans perceive as routine research must be adjusted to South African social realities.

Telephone surveys are also unpredictable. Few people have phones; thus research is restricted to the upper classes. Urban males who own phones are rarely home. Their wives or servants, who do not always speak English, rarely respond well to phone calls from strangers. Message taking is rare. Static overrides conversation; storms cut service altogether.

Home surveys may be sketchy and sporadic. Maps may be outdated, unavailable, or nonexistent. Street signs and addresses may not exist. A house may contain one family or several, or a fluctuating group of transients, or a pack of guard dogs. Tsotsi gangs make evening interviews unsafe. Yet, adults may work six days a week and only be at home at night, or they may work night shifts and sleep all day. Sundays are spent at church or visiting. In short, this method may yield little data.

Even conversation is unpredictable. African speaking styles differ from ours; they can have different goals. We like directness; they love oratory. We seek accuracy; they want agreement. We want the truth or the facts; they want to avoid conflict. As a result, potential informants may provide only those opinions they feel you want to hear.

They may also avoid specifics. Remember that Bantu tradition perceives verbal precision not merely as bad form but also as the catalyst of subsequent misfortune. We see vague answers as evasion; they see them as good manners.

To test this conversational style, deliberately get lost, then ask passersby repeatedly just how far you are from an intended destination. Usually, the reply is "not far." The response is neither wrong nor sufficiently specific to be useful. Informants may not want to disappoint you by providing actual data, since they often mean to help you reach your destination by leading you in person. This pattern of response applies to marketing queries as well. Expect agreement and kindness but neither accuracy nor precision.

Why Research On-Site?

There are professional reasons for you to personally research a potential marketing site. One is the chance to develop a degree of local intuition. The decision to interact with clientele does more than merely supplement your secondary data. It also reduces the psychological distance between you and your targeted population, allowing you to move beyond merely measuring their commercial needs and begin to sense them as individuals (Goodyear 1982).

On-site interviews also create on-site business insights and opportunities. In Zimbabwe, for instance, I once met cast members from The Peoples' Road Show, a group employed to market Christianity and commerce. Sponsors paid to have their goods extolled throughout the townships in gospel rhythms, interspersed with sermons, drums, and trumpets. It is a uniquely African way to spread a marketing message, and one I find effective—but I can write about it only because I was there to watch it work.

On-site interviewing can also help you modify your message to fit local sensibilities. Consider Coca-Cola's fate, for instance, when launching Mello Yello (a soft drink) in the townships at a time when residents fought frequently with white police. Mello Yello delivery vans were shaped like rounded soft-drink cans and painted green and yellow. Police used rounded, yellow armored cars against the rioters. Township crowds stoned them all, thereby linking Mello Yello to police and apartheid (Morris). Here, a single on-site researcher might have seen the similarity, grasped the township mood, and suggested changing both product name and vehicle design. No one did and the product failed.

There are also professional reasons to conduct your on-site research with African staff. One is simply to conform to local custom. A Bantu proverb, heard across South Africa, declares,

> [Anyone] who walks alone must be a witch.

The saying is based on two beliefs. One is that when anyone walks (or works) in solitude, it is with intent to harm. The other is that a person only reaches full potential with the aid of others. One often hears the Zulu proverb:

> *Umuntu ngumuntu ngabantu* (A person is a
> person through people).

It basically means "No man is an island." In South Africa, no entrepreneur can be an island. To reach full commercial potential in South Africa means working with others—which should include African staff.

A second reason to employ Africans is to conform to South African law. The employment of Africans is required by government directive. Since 1994 affirmative action programs have expanded exponentially. Blacks have virtually replaced Whites at executive and managerial levels within national, provincial, _ and municipal ministries as well as in the judiciary, army, and police.

The private sector is required to follow suit. Amalgamated Banks of South Africa, for instance, plans to Africanize no less than 70 percent of its staff. Such swift, dramatic strides are expected of everyone. Your refusal to hire African staff will draw queries from both government departments and local unions. They may ask how many Africans you plan to hire, your employment criteria, what posts they will hold, and under what conditions they will work. Most important, they will ask how many you intend to advance to managerial levels and how soon (Cadman 1999). Prudence suggests you prepare your answers thoughtfully.

A final reason to hire Africans is to ensure your personal acceptance among those with whom you plan to work. This goes beyond satisfying the demands of union and government officials to how you will be received among potential clientele. Few foreigners do well when they work alone within communal cultures. To be accepted by those who equate solitude with witchcraft, it is wise to work with a team, and preferably with team members your informants know.

On a personal level, African staff who live in areas you plan to research can facilitate your safety. Professionally, they can provide linguistic, cultural, and commercial advice as well as introductions. Commercially, they are more likely than you to spot existing demand, emerging trends, and potential competitors. Socially, you can obligate older local notables by hiring younger family or clan members. In short, it makes sense to employ African staff.

Whom to Hire

Start by hiring a single research team for on-site marketing research. Train them first to work within one area where they are known, whether rural, urban, or township. As they gain experience, you can either shift the group to a second area or use it to train new teams. Consider where your informants will work when deciding which sex to hire. In the field, male interviewers work best with male informants; female staff, when interviewing women. Office staff have no contact with informants, and can be of either gender. For now, assume this team will be male. The group you first hire will include the following individuals:

- *An interviewer.* This individual will identify, locate, and interact directly with informants. When you join the team, he translates for you. When the team works without you, he conducts the interviews. He must be younger than the informants. Bantu tradition dictates that the young learn from the old. He should also be extroverted, an excellent conversationalist, fluent in the local dialects, and widely connected in the area to be investigated.

- *A prober/recorder.* This person handles tape recorders during interviews. He must also be skilled at repairing them, since they often break down. As the interviewer questions an informant, the prober listens. Periodically, he interrupts to probe more deeply, injecting secondary questions to elicit more detailed responses. The ideal prober, therefore, should be serious, reflective, and somewhat introverted. Since he, too, is to learn from informants, he must be younger than they.

- *A transcriber and a translator.* These two are from your office staff. The first transcribes the collected data in the informant's language. The second translates it into English. Both also serve as analysts in that they are encouraged to add in the margins written comments to what informants and interviewers say. Since neither is on-site, they can consider what is said with more detachment, paying heed to underlying meanings. Ideally, they should be older (and/ or female), thus providing different perspectives from those of the younger men in the field. Over time, their comments will take on increasing value, both to you and to them. As both office analysts gain experience, the chance to give advice provides them with increasing interest in what would otherwise be routine recording work.

- *A driver/mechanic.* This man is a driver, mechanic, and researcher. Hire him not only for vehicle expertise but also for area knowledge. He should know each route in a proposed research zone and either make or already have contacts in each neighborhood. His research role is to learn where threats may occur and keep the team away from danger. While others interview, he guards the car; if danger threatens, he drives them away.

When interviewing applicants for your research team, adapt your hiring criteria to local lifestyles. Ask applicants to which factions (clan, guild, church, etc.) they belong and what each group might do for you. Alternately, hire selected staff at the request of others; if an important contact asks you to consider someone, do so regardless of qualifications. Remember, *both* will subsequently owe you favors. Alternately, hire members of a clan, ideally drawing employees from one extended family. Here, peer pressure, family loyalty, and clan honor can ensure high levels of responsibility. Finally, hire women (again, ideally from one clan). If divorced or dependent on indifferent spouses, they seek independence through employment. Few are unionized, regarding unions as male. All belong to extensive families, work hard, accept responsibility, and can delight in work away from home.

Motivating Your Interview Staff

Motivate these new employees in ways that reflect South African realities. American managers often motivate staff solely by offering what they feel are fair wages for good work. However, South African managers often complain that employees quit their jobs once they earn enough money to meet immediate needs. This suggests that fair pay alone is not enough.

Consider the question of pay from a worker's perspective. All South African wages are low by American standards, but no one agrees on how high they should be. As a result, Africans feel massively underpaid and thus exploited, especially if they compare their living standards with yours (Shabulala 1996). You can, nonetheless, take steps to create satisfaction. One is to pay more than staff can earn doing similar work elsewhere. Better still, offer more than wages; supplement pay with perks. Pick up the cost of public transport between your workers' homes and work. Provide tasty, visually appealing worksite food, especially meat, thus presenting what your staff may consider a luxury. Even serving unlimited tea, milk, sugar, and coffee may be a luxury, since few African firms provide them. Your extra costs may be repaid by peace of mind.

Offer these employees new status. Give each an appropriate and impressive job title in English. I use "Research Associate." Reinforce this by presenting staff with individual business cards, bearing their title and the logo of your firm. Among their peers, both titles and cards reflect status. Thereafter, invite each to buy a new business suit at company expense. Fine clothes convey not only dignity but unity, which is useful where people value belonging to groups. Suits also bring status, since the very act of wearing them will advertise they are employed.

Offer your staff new skills, which both facilitate your work and advance their careers. One obvious example is American business English; they should be trained in both writing and speaking. A less obvious example is financial management. Employees may lack any experience in handling their own financial affairs—dealing with banks, ATMs, credit cards, and so forth. Where these gaps exist, fill them. Thereafter, teach them how the research skills they will be learning (interviewing, data analysis, report writing, etc.) will prove useful, both in later stages of your project and in their subsequent careers.

Finally, offer them a new horizon; the chance of promotion. Explain that each job may lead to a better one as the project expands. Americans consider this self-evident. Africans may not. Under apartheid, promotion was almost unheard of. One job was usually for life. Even now, when black political power has raised the expectations of the educated elite who now rise within firms, millions still work without hope of advancement. Counter this by telling staff you have not merely hired them as researchers, drivers, and so on, but also as potential marketers and managers. As the project advances, so can they, assuming new tasks after relevant training. Provide no guarantees, but offer more than a job. Suggest a career.

Effective Interviewing

Most overseas managers face several problems in training research staff to interview effectively. The most immediate is to teach newly employed team members to link personal appearance with professionalism. Remember, they may be young men with limited education in business protocol. Teach them why the business suits they buy must be conservative in cut and color. Explain why sunglasses and certain personal ornaments (e.g., chains, multiple rings) suggest a gangster image. Describe how shoes must be maintained in mud or dusty regions. Discuss the use of business cards as well as etiquette for smoking. In short, define and justify the image these men must cultivate to gain professional acceptance.

Train new staff to seek out contacts who may be *professionally* useful, rather than simply individuals to whom they are related or who live nearby. I teach a technique used by a British colleague each time he enters South Africa on business:

> I search out the most famous and knowledgeable
> man I can realistically reach, and by socializing
> with his circle of friends I gradually discover
> others who can be of greater use. The point is to
> aim high, make friends, then move up even
> higher. (Cadman)

Apply this concept to your team. Specify a future research zone. Ask each team member who he knows personally and considers knowledgeable, powerful, and potentially useful, and in each case, ask why. If team members know no one in the designated area, send them out to learn who does. I once told a newly hired research team to locate the very oldest men and women in six different mountain regions. Knowing no one outside their own areas, they fanned out to find people who did. Your field staff can do the same.

The greatest problem is to instruct each trainee to master his role during interviews. Teach your interviewer that introductions must be factual, despite African traditions that call for oratory. The team leader must present you (name, position, firm), describe the point of your visit, and emphasize that you come to ask advice.

Train him to be flexible while asking questions, rather than either quoting yours from memory or reading woodenly from a list. He must both rephrase basic questions as circumstances dictate and add his own. In this type of interviewing informant feedback determines where the conversation goes, and he must be prepared to deviate from any script. This can be difficult, since deviation from written documents goes against what is learned in South African schools, where memorization is rewarded, rote reading is a learning goal, and ad-libbing is punished.

Teach the prober to be curious. This can also prove difficult, as he must overcome both schooling and tradition. The young do not traditionally probe elders' wisdom but listen passively as they are taught. As a result, probing must be taught, and it will take practice. Have both team members practice first with you, then have them interview older Africans on staff. Thereafter, let them try their skills on strangers.

Teach tape-recording techniques. No data are worthwhile unless recorded. Your team must learn to look for quiet meeting places where recording is possible. Once there, the prober must learn how best to gain permission for the recorder to be used. (Informants often initially object.) This is best achieved by first recording and then replaying your voice in conversation with informants, and then by offering them copies of the final tape. Should it break in midinterview, the prober must either substitute another or take notes to fill the gap. However, since note taking is not taught in schools, training may be needed here as well.

Train yourself. When you interview, your primary problem will be to motivate informants to the point where they talk freely. Never offer money, gifts, or product samples. They can magically transform informants into employees who then provide whatever data they decide will please a newfound foreign boss. Thereafter, as gossip spreads, everyone with whom you speak will ask for pay. There are better alternatives. Remember that you can also do favors, placing recipients in your debt. You may ask a local notable to intervene on your behalf. Finally, as often mentioned, consider socializing. The round of drinks you buy can override both shyness and mistrust.

Effective Questions

Phrasing questions so as to elicit maximum data poses additional problems. Begin by writing out each question in English, wording it to stimulate discussion rather than one-word replies (i.e., avoid questions that can be answered with yes or no). Ask two of your staff to translate the questions into the language that will be used to interview. Finally, ask the other two to translate them back into English, without looking at your original wording. This last step may cause heated staff debates, but subsequent adjustments of the final wording should both be precise and provide more useful data.

A second problem concerns the order in which questions should be asked. Offer your staff four guidelines:

1. Begin with warm-ups. Since even knowledgeable informants may initially be shy, start simply. Ask each informant how he or she became commercially established. Then ask what difficulties were overcome along the way. Most people gladly recount their troubles and triumphs, then relax and take pleasure in your subsequent queries.

2. Query chronologically (or sequentially), moving step by step, from start to finish of whatever business process you explore. If this seems obvious to you, it can be less so to staff and informants, who may follow other rules of both chronology and logic. Consequently, you must enforce the order in which questions proceed, in order to keep conversations on track.

3. Ask open-ended questions (those beginning with *why, where, what, when,* and *how*) that require explanations rather than yes or no replies. Thus the query "What might happen if…" will elicit more data than asking "Would this work?"

4. Ask for one answer at a time, so as not to confuse informants. A question eliciting a single answer ("What is the greatest risk if we offer this product?") will elicit a more focused response than one that asks for several ("What problems will we have if…").

Display real products to stimulate discussion. Many respondents prefer to analyze a product they are holding over one they must remember or imagine. They may also wish to discuss products they know from the past or in the present rather than speculate on a future one (Goodyear).

Debrief your team as each interview day ends. Ask what they think and feel about each informant and what they learned from each interview. Ask what went right, what went wrong, and why. Often, their comments will surprise you. I once expressed my delight in the information provided by an informant. My African staff declared they had enjoyed it too, because they knew the man was drunk and fantasizing as we went along. Take written notes on the opinions your field staff provide. Their comments grow in value over time, as interviewer and prober both gain experience and start to realize that their opinions actually do matter.

Delays, Disagreements, and Drunks

Delay is the problem most frequently encountered in the field, due either to an informant's late arrival or his failure to arrive at all. Unfortunately, groups of spectators often gather to stare silently as you wait. Rather than feeling awkward or immobilized, spend the waiting time interviewing one (or several) of them, then shift attention back to your intended informant when that person appears. Often, such spontaneous street interviews will be more useful than data from a more established source.

Spectators may also pose a problem by disagreeing with informants. All too often, you must converse in settings where an informant must both express opinions and be heard by members of a watching crowd. African etiquette allows passersby to stop and listen without feeling they intrude; thus your interviews may quickly become public. Unfortunately, etiquette also allows listeners to disagree with your informant, displaying reactions that can range from simple laughter to derisive shouts and counterarguments from every side. In such cases, quiet the crowd and ask them to select a spokesman. Usually, they will select the oldest person in the group and will listen silently to his comments. If you then end the interview, they will disperse. Then you can pick up your conversation with the original informant at another time and place.

Your team must finally deal with the problem of alcohol. To be effective, informants must be sober—as must those who crowd around to listen. Nevertheless, you may arrive at an appointed place to find informants, spectators, or both partially drunk. To minimize this possibility, interview early in the day; avoid late afternoons and evenings. If offered drinks on arrival, sip slowly and train your field staff to match your consumption rate. If alcohol significantly impairs an informant's ideas, terminate the interview with a promise to return. Or consider the commercial benefits of staying on awhile to socialize. You might learn more in conversation than by interviewing.

Writing (Biased?) Reports

For maximum value, your written reports should contain both factual data and subjective impressions. However, beware of bias; there are three types that may distort your writing.

You are the first and most dangerous. Beware of your personal project bias. Overseas managers want their projects to succeed and thus may select informants (and phrase questions) so as to produce the conclusions they want. Consider your bias regarding security; will it force you to research "antiseptically" by restricting contact to informants in safe areas and familiar situations. Watch out, too, for gender bias, where you speak only with men or women. Beware of elitist bias, where you focus on urban, English-speaking informants, reasoning that only the elite can offer valid data. Finally, beware of anthropological bias, where your own desire to explore the exotic may outweigh your actual business needs (Goodyear).

Your team may form a second source of bias, based on their religion, kin, clan, and tribe. Remember that field staff may try to restrict your interviews to kinsmen, tribesmen, and fellow worshippers rather than strangers who might prove more informative. A team once did that to me, simply by failing to mention that each informant had the same clan name, no matter where we went. When I learned what was happening, I could tell they had no idea why I was displeased. Employees may also keep you away from those they regard as traditional enemies. Two researchers once spent so much time depicting people in one faction as hostile that I finally queried a respected elder. I then learned that the group in question was hostile to my staff, not me. In consequence, I hired new researchers from that region to work with me while I was there.

Your informants, of course, provide the third source of bias. Remember to discount sources who offer only what they feel you want to hear. Beware of personal pride, where informants extol their own business achievements while depicting clients and competitors as dolts. Consider racial pride, which may appear when Westernized informants provide more optimistic views than actually exist ("We have no bribery here"). Watch out for pride in Western ways; some European-trained informants are so alienated from tribal custom as to despise traditional lifestyles and denigrate traditional markets. Beware of tribal pride; it colors each group's view of the others. I once met a Tswana who had worked with Zulu in the gold mines. I asked how both groups got on together. His answer was brief: "When we met, we fought."

There is no antidote for bias; it will inevitably tinge your reports. If you doubt an informant, ask your staff to evaluate him. When in doubt about staff, ask African colleagues. If you are unsure of yourself, keep interviewing until you can predict the answers. Only then can you become sufficiently secure to draw conclusions.

Your on-site reports should be concrete, detailed, and specific, discussing real locations, situations, and people. The Third World has no time for abstract theory. Each concrete step you advocate should be accompanied by specific reasons to carry it out. Beyond that, what you write can also add color, movement, excitement, and life to the picture you draw of a developing market as well as the options now offered your firm. In short, the report should not be based on marketing abstractions but on firsthand knowledge. At this point in the project, that means your organization will have developed three assets: your written conclusions, an effective African staff, and you.

References

Boyd, Harper W., Jr., Ronald E. Frank, William F. Massy, and Mostafa Zoheir. 1964. "On the Use of Marketing Research in the Emerging Economies." *Journal of Marketing Research* 1, no. 4 (November): 20–23.

Cadman, Anthony G. Chairman, Anthony Cadman Associates, South Africa. 1999. Personal conversations.

Erikson, Leo. 1986. "Analyzing the Brazilian Consumers Market." *Business Topics* 2 (Summer): 7–26.

Goodyear, Mary. 1982. "Qualitative Research in Developing Countries." *Journal of the Market Research Society* 24, no. 2 (April): 86–96.

Lepage, Francoise. 1989. "Americans Simply Harm Themselves by Not Boning Up on Cultures of Others." *San Francisco Business Times* (30 October), 25.

Morris, Robin. 1992. *Marketing to Black Townships: Practical Guidelines*. Cape Town: Juta & Co., 30, 36, 41, 42.

Shabulala, Dume. Labor leader, COSATU. 1996. Radio debate with Dr. Anthony Cadman, KwaZulu-Natal (23 April).

7

Marketing to Peasant Clientele

Peasant: 1. a small farmer or farm laborer; 2. a
usually uneducated person of low social status.
—*Merriam Webster's Collegiate Dictionary*

Despite their poverty, peasants have always
formed an immense market for the products
manufactured by multinational corporations.
With current world population at 5.3 billion,
peasants in just the less developed countries
number 2.8 billion...[y]et...are not targeted as a
special market segment by [these] firms.
—Hendrick Serrie

Perhaps some urban firms do research rural
needs. Nonetheless, existing literature provides
many examples of firms that do not.... Executive
decision makers may not only remain unaware of
peasant...needs, but rarely even wonder about
them...just as peasants rarely wonder about the
needs of corporate executives.
—Jeffrey Fadiman

Having developed an effective research team, you will want to
evaluate specific segments of your potential clientele. Do not
ignore the peasants. Many American executives feel this group
lacks the interest, knowledge, and money to buy what they
sell. As one overseas manager expressed it: "Peasants don't
buy [our] pharmaceuticals. That's why we don't march up and

down the countryside and market to them. Our line is sophisticated. They're not."

Ignoring Rural Clientele

South African peasants, whether subsistence farmers or farm laborers, make up 76.4 percent of the black population (Trade Union Research Project [TURP] 1994). This seems too large an economic segment to ignore. Nonetheless, we often do just that, focusing solely on existing urban markets. Some CEOs bypass peasant clientele because their employees lack rural expertise. Such firms are urban based, urban staffed, and urban oriented. Unlike Russian or Chinese managers, who often rise from rural origins, U.S. executives are often urban born, urban educated, and therefore urbanized. That mindset leads them to develop urban product lines designed to meet needs that peasants do not share. Urban dwellers, for example, value labor-saving products. Peasants feel more labor leads to greater reward, thus providing higher status. In consequence, few peasants flock to purchase labor-saving goods.

America's high-tech mindset may also cause us to ignore this low-tech clientele. We perceive more complex products as more useful, thus more salable. Consider Apple's personal computers, which have evolved from user-friendly to user-confusing, as the firm develops ever more sophisticated features (used by ever fewer clients) as well as massive service centers to handle queries as to how they work: "I tried to explain the problem to the techno-snob: 'You have a series *three*?' she asked incredulously, 'We're into series six now'" (Janis 1997).

High-tech marketers argue that complex, urban-oriented goods will simply trickle out of urban centers into adjacent rural areas. They feel urban and rural needs are similar; both groups buy aspirin for a headache or matches to light fires. In fact, their needs are different. While rural and urban buyers may want similar goods, they need them in different forms and quantities. Thus, Durban's urban pharmacies sell aspirin in bottles of fifty. KwaZulu peasants buy them in units of one.

Some Americans shun rural markets because they find them personally disconcerting. They prefer to filter rural experiences through a screen of modern comforts. Thus, tourists in South African wilderness regions prefer to view their wildlife through the windows of a safari vehicle or lodge, subordinating the wildness to their comfort. Rural South Africa is not geared to comfort. Electricity fails; cars fall prey to washboard roads; mosquitos swarm at sundown; dog packs howl at night; and roosters crow at dawn, precluding rest.

Nor is rural life commercially predictable. Contacts can be late or fail to appear for meetings. Goods awaiting pickup overheat in the baking sun. Flash floods upset tight schedules. Scheduled bus departures can not only be postponed but also "pre-poned," when drivers decide to leave early without waiting for passengers. Taxi-vans leave only when the vehicle is full. Phone calls make callers want to "reach out and hit someone," as service is erratic. In short, these areas are poorly organized for U.S. business.

Finally, Americans may look down on peasant clientele. As noted at the beginning of this chapter, the word *peasant* has two meanings in our language: a small farmer or farm laborer and/or an uneducated person of low social status (*Merriam Webster's Collegiate Dictionary* 1997). We often hold these stereotypes, perhaps unconsciously, defining peasant market segments as composed of poor, uneducated, and cloddish consumers who are both unaware of Western goods and lacking funds to buy them. "We go into places so poor that the experts say there is no purchasing power" (Millman 1991, 80).

When things go wrong in rural regions, uncertainties are created that make it harder for overseas managers to either produce or predict results. Even so, their American-based supervisors demand reliable predictions and specified results. In consequence, home office expectations create anxiety for those on-site. Often, it seems safer to merely focus on familiar urban markets, where predictable results seem more assured. The less familiar peasant markets offer greater risks. That can mean, however, that these potentially profitable market segments will be ignored simply because we have not yet learned how—or why—to approach them.

Why Peasant Markets?

Peasants make good customers, and they do want Western goods. One excellent reason to consider this vast clientele is its striking uniformity. Whether the market site is in Zulu, Sotho, Xhosa, Tswana, or Venda areas, the image is the same: primarily female vendors offering a narrow range of near-identical products with minimal packaging, rudimentary display, shifting prices, and no promotion. Swazi, Sotho, and Tswana alike seek products that are small, sold in single units, and low-priced; they want products that do not break and that produce real (or imagined) change when put to use. Thus, soap must clean; candles must burn; iodine must sting. When the products perform as expected, these clients buy again.

Subsistence farmers across South Africa seek similar services. They want products that entertain and break the monotony of their work. Peasants in rural Venda, Tsonga, and Ndebele alike want radios, tape decks, and Walkmans. They also seek mobility. Since work binds them to one patch of land, they want to go elsewhere, so an untapped market exists for machines that move and carry loads. Men ride bicycles, but women still walk, often bearing burdens on their heads. A four-wheeled feminine variant—small, light, flexible, easily repairable—would help them negotiate the rutted paths with heavy loads. The demand is there.

Peasants, too, seek similar sources of status. American goods can provide these status symbols—though the peasants often use the goods in ways unanticipated by producers. One Swazi acquaintance gains status simply from wearing an American watch, though he cannot tell time. One Tswana contact gains status from owning an American TV, though his home lacks electricity. My former neighbors, Zulu farm workers, gain status from the American college sweatshirts they wear while cutting sugarcane, despite the searing heat. This type of demand occurs too often to ignore.

A second reason to enter rural markets is the degree to which this clientele now *generates* demand for Western goods and services through exposure to the media. Peasants make good customers because they know just what they want. Demand is created in rural South Africa, as in rural America, by watching or hearing commercials on radio and TV. One coastal clan I know works in reed-thatched huts, carving statues for the tourist trade while listening to daily radio reports on the fluctuating prices of the wood they import from Mozambique. High Veld farmers gather in crossroads general stores that sell everything from matches to nails to beer. The real attraction, however, is standing together for hours before the TV, watching programs and commercials from *Egoli* (Johannesburg). Inevitably, both the media and the messages create demand.

Finally, peasants make good customers because they have purchasing power. We perceive them as poor, because farm incomes are low. We thus assume they have too little to spend on foreign goods. We also view potential customers as individuals, rather than members of communal groups. It is true that one isolated, rural family may have too little income to purchase much or often—but rural families do not live in isolation. Like cash-short Americans, they have access to informal lines of credit. As noted earlier, peasants can acquire capital through extended-family and rotation funding. A third source has also just begun to function in South Africa: microfunding.

Microfunding began in 1982, when Mohammed Yunis launched the Grameen Bank in Bangladesh. His initial purpose was to offer loans to those excluded by Western banks, but half of the nation's population qualified. He then ruled that only the poorest would be eligible. Finally, since men control the wealth in Bangladesh, he further restricted loans to women (Bornstein 1995; Yunis 1997).

Grameen has seven rules. Start-up loans are small, ranging from twenty to one hundred dollars. Repayment starts in seven days, with tiny sums to be repaid each week. However, interest charges are four points above commercial rates. Each repayment must be prompt and complete. No collateral is required from recipients; instead, each must join (or be part of) a five-member group composed of friends or kin. Each group must join a forty-member center. All center members must attend a financial meeting each week to learn how money can be used. Most important, each member must assume responsibility for the loans of all other group members. One person's default blocks future loans for everyone; thus peer pressure becomes a primary financial tool. Prompt payment gains the group access to further credit.

Grameen binds clientele by offering them supplementary services. The centers start by teaching members how to save. Once stable savings accounts have been established, members may qualify for new loans, low-cost seeds, ducks, reading lessons, and financial consultation. No service is free—a key element in convincing borrowers to respect both the services and the provider. Repayment rates average 98 percent, with two million clients having received loans of $2.3 billion. Loans are expected to approach $500 million (Mathews 1993; James 1998).

Microfunding has reached Africa. Senegalese microloans are provided by Catholic Relief Services. In Ghana, the Woman's World Working Bank, operating out of an open market in Accra, uses only female staff to microfinance female clientele. In Zimbabwe and South Africa, a U.S.-sponsored private firm, Trickle Up, launches rural ventures by providing starter loans of $50 (Dixon 1999). Where capital is made available, rural consumers will not only borrow, they will buy.

Researching Rural Demand

One way to determine product demand among peasants is simply to ask them; there is no substitute for on-site conversation. A second method is to research commercial aspects of their recent history. In the past, white administrators of the tribal reserves often wrote about quite unexpected peasant responses to Western innovations. In some cases, these administrators required Africans to construct hundreds of cement toilets. However, no one used them as the manufacturers intended, converting them instead to storage bins to protect their valued grain from rats, birds, snakes, and insects. The consistency of these historical narratives suggests a need for products (aside from toilets!) that improve food storage and pest control. No doubt additional analysis of rural histories will offer other options.

Another way to learn what peasants want is to analyze their current use of Western products. Zulu children, for instance, have created an unanticipated market for wire coat hangers. They twine them together to make toy cars, trucks, and planes with moving wire wheels. Each time I traveled outside my home area to the nearest city, local children asked me to return with hangers. A U.S. toy firm should tap this demand instead.

Demand can also be determined by learning how peasant women use traditional products. Filipino women, for instance, use juice from a local fruit to wash their clothes, valuing it for both its pleasant scent and its stain-removing qualities. Procter and Gamble researchers refined the concept, developing a laundry bar that contained the juice, duplicated the scent, and named it for the fruit (Beckett 1990). The product succeeded, thus suggesting that analyzing how women use South African plants might open further markets. In KwaZulu alone, over four hundred indigenous medicinal plants are regularly harvested, processed, and sold to traditional healers by an estimated five hundred women gleaners (Cunningham 1991). They have much to teach potential marketers.

Demand can also be inferred by examining traditional religion and customs, particularly how Western products can be used in local practices. Compare the various ways to use a pack of cigarettes: if we buy them, we mean to smoke them. If Africans buy them, they smoke some but give most to those they meet; the cigarette is used to trigger fellowship and conversation. However, cigarettes can also be religious offerings. In Northern Province, for instance, certain huge trees are still sacred to the ancestors. They were traditionally adorned with offerings of meat. Nowadays, one often sees them hung with cigarettes. Could other Western products meet related spiritual needs?

Religious analysis can also make Western products more acceptable to rural clientele. In Zimbabwe, for example, an agrochemical firm introduced a range of herbicides into a rural Shona region. However, no one asked permission of the *masvikiro* (spirit-mediums), who provide religious guidance through rites that maintain contact with the Shona ancestors. Ignored by the company, the Shona rose up against the project, arguing that its chemicals poisoned the earth, thereby angering the ancestors. The Western managers aborted the program (Creekmore 1986). Research into the Shona religion would have taught them which rituals would have purified the product line, making it acceptable to Shona clientele.

Finally, you can learn what peasants want by watching current rural enterprises. Often, these innovators respond to Western trends with ventures of their own. Examining them may suggest unanticipated commercial possibilities. Consider these:

In Chad rural entrepreneurs developed "tabletop petrol stops" to compete with French corporate gas stations. Entrepreneurs buy petrol from both legal and illegal sources and resell it in containers from the tops of folding tables. Hand-lettered signs advertise each enterprise; wine jugs hold gasoline, and gin flasks hold motor oil. Mechanics are available on request. These entrepreneurs' success lies in flexible pricing, which drops below the corporate competition in daylight but rises at dusk, when the French stations close (Kraft 1987). Many South African gas stations now close at dusk. Success in Chad suggests that a moonlight option might also work in South Africa.

In Zimbabwe one women's group has tapped a children's market. Uniting to generate demand, they approached 120 primary schools with offers to sew the hundreds of identical school uniforms children must wear to attend. Since children must often walk miles to reach school, they also offered to sew sets of identical sandals (Creekmore). Their boldness certainly suggests a similar market for school wear among South Africa's children.

In KwaZulu, the Obanjeni (Zulu) Women's Cooperative has developed two quite different markets for hats: one for rural fashion, another for skin protection. Obanjeni turns pollution into profit. Plastic shopping bags blow endlessly across their fields, dangling from every fence and thornbush. The women gather, clean, and slice them, and then weave the slices into whatever will sell. One hundred bags will make a mat; twenty-five become a stylish hat (Naidoo 1995). To stimulate demand, the women now blend fashion with concern for health. They advertise the hats as sun protectors, since skin cancer is increasing among Zulu.

Creating Rural Demand

Rural demand can also be created. Consider the experience of four small firms, each of which now generates demand by modifying either African or Western products in ways that meet specific rural needs.

The Freeplay Group of Cape Town has decided that demand can be created for no-maintenance products. With limited income, potential buyers fear postpurchase costs. Think about the radio from this perspective. Where rural areas lack electricity, radios need batteries—frequently, since they often play all night. Freeplay has modified this product for rural use by devising a windup radio with a metal crank. Crank it and the radio gets AM, FM, and shortwave (Dahle 1999). That means every rural homestead can tap into the information age without recurring battery costs. No-maintenance goods mean rural sales.

Jua Kali (Hot Sun), a Kenya group, believes demand can be created for goods that cut rural household costs. Look, for example, at the traditional African cookstove from the perspective of a rural homestead on limited income. Cooking with wood creates two long-range costs. One comes from buying the wood, since many South African peasants have no forests near their homes. The second is the cost in health. Three stones make up a fireplace, on which one puts an iron pot. However, only ten percent of a fire's heat reaches both pot and food. The rest goes into the air as methane, carbon dioxide, and particles that combine with both gases to create lung and eye infections (Kammen 1995). In time, the resulting health care needs will drive up household costs.

Jua Kali has modified the cookstove concept to deal with both problems. It combines the iron casing of a traditional cook pot with a ceramic insulating liner that captures up to 40 percent of a fire's heat, thus cutting cooking time. A hole is cut in the side, through the ceramic/iron casing, in which the cook lays sticks of wood so that only the ends are exposed to flame. As a result, the sticks burn more slowly. Shorter cooking time and slow burning mean less wood (thirteen hundred pounds less wood, per family, per year) is used, thus cutting costs for buying wood up to 20 percent (Kammen). Thus far, Jua Kali's *kuni mbili* (two-stick) stoves have been selling well in Kenya. If we provide them, South Africans might buy similar products that cut the costs of both illness and fuel.

Natal's Group Five Trans-Africa (G5) knows that peasants want solid shelter and believes demand can be created for low-cost, rainproof homes. Traditional homesteads are vulnerable to South Africa's seasonal rains, which can be so intense that they not only penetrate thatch roofs but also dissolve the mud-brick walls. You will recall that former President Mandela promised modern homes to every African, but progress is slow and many of those built were substandard and quickly collapsed. G5 responded by developing ways to construct a modern, rainproof home in just one week. The homes are small by U.S. standards but are so solid that G5 gives all buyers a hammer and invites them to destroy what they have built. They fail.

G5 dwellings are constructed from steel molds filled with concrete spray that encapsulates prelaid plumbing and electric wires. As the concrete dries, the molds are removed to use on the next house. Financing is available to groups of people who decide to live as neighbors. They pool funds to collectively acquire land, subsidies, and building loans. In rural communities, rainproof roofs, functional plumbing, and stable electricity provide status. To offer them means sales (Van der Walt 1996).

Traansvaal's Afrika Bakery, Ltd., first established solely to provide jobs for returning ANC freedom fighters, decided to create demand for African fast food. The firm has evolved from a standard bread-producing bakery into a training-oriented business that plans to set up two hundred African-owned, franchised bakeries to sell bread across the High Veld. However, its profits now come less from bread than from training fees and commercial consultation with potential franchisees (Mnyanda 1996). Its success suggests a larger market in hot fast food for rural laborers who rise at dawn.

These four firms have similarities worth noting. First, they are small, with limited capital; they cannot buy their way into a market. Second, they work on-site with clientele, to discern both short- and long-term needs. Once established, they create demand by devising new ways to do old things.

Unconventional Market Entry

Rural market entry may require unconventional methods. In the United States, conventional marketing practice calls for consumer surveys to determine what is needed and how much clients will pay to meet these needs. In South Africa, this method can create negative perceptions of the seller. This is particularly true in today's political climate, where white businessmen who use standard Western business practices can now be accused of exploiting black clientele.

One less conventional option is to sponsor existing rural production. For example, in Thailand in the 1950s weaving raw silk was a peasant industry. Some weavers migrated to Bangkok, forming villages on its edges. They used hand looms to produce a few yards of silk per day. Jim Thompson, an American businessman, collected samples of their work. He sold them in hotels, approaching tourists with silks draped artfully over his shoulders. Soon, his increasing flow of orders provided work for every weaving clan on the outskirts of the city.

Thompson then transformed his role from buyer to sponsor. He offered the weavers loans to buy more looms to increase production. Next, he proposed improvements in the weaving process: Swiss colorfast dyes replaced Thai ones. Bright American colors replaced soft Thai shades. Thai designs were reshaped to Western tastes. Looms were modified to increase their speed. Notwithstanding, the economic changes were so gradual that the weavers' social structure was unchanged. Thompson refused suggestions to install the weavers in factories. He had no wish to Westernize them, just to sponsor what they wove (Warren 1983).

By first finding a niche, then reshaping a peasant industry to fill it, Thompson became Thailand's Silk King. His method can be useful in South Africa. There is a tourist market, for instance, for artistically designed products made out of South Africa's luxurious Karroo wool. Many Karroo cooperatives weave traditional designs into thick woolen rugs. Artistically, the results are striking, but the weavers live too far from the tourist routes to generate demand.

A U.S. sponsor could help them modernize their methods, adapt their product lines to Western tastes, and market the results in Western ways. Designs could expand to include surrealistic scenes from local African mythology. Production could diversify from the currently produced rugs to stylish shawls, capes, sweaters, coats, and dresses—each with mythological scenes worked into the wool. Markets could be developed along the normal tourist stops, or the cooperatives themselves could become tourist destinations. Clearly, this type of sponsorship could bring profit to both sides.

A foreign sponsor may also opt to dramatize rural skills, transforming traditional activities into a mutually profitable tourist attraction. This method goes beyond a mere display of crafts to the presentation of traditional life—from herding to cooking to healing to dance—as a learning experience for foreign visitors. Participants essentially change careers, transforming themselves from subsistence farmers into actors in a corporate-sponsored play in which aspects of their work are performed for tourists. Performers receive wages from the sponsor, thereby entering the wage economy. Most important, members of every age group from infants to elders gain employment, which can involve entire clans at little cost.

This type of sponsorship is now used in KwaZulu. One hotel employed subsistence farmers to construct a traditional Zulu village on its land. It was to be a historical attraction, a stage on which to present the Zulu past. Anthropologists, historians, and local elders conducted training. Traditional behavior was modified to meet Western expectations (e.g., American tourists smile during a formal greeting; traditionally, the Zulu did not). Those who spoke English became narrators, explaining the traditions on which displays were based. All others became actors, taking pride in the chance to relive Zulu tradition.

Today, the re-created village is alive. Healers, hut builders, and herders demonstrate their work. Men exhibit carvings, women display weavings, and children show off wire toys. Cooks and brewers provide Zulu food and beer. Singers, drummers, and dancers entertain. Narrators offer continuity and depth. The sponsors offer lodging in Zulu beehive huts with Westernized interiors. The result is a sponsored re-creation of past and present rural skills that proves profitable to both Zulu participants and the firm.

The boldest option would be to sponsor an entire community, transforming its economic structure from subsistence farming into business ventures that complement your firm's commercial needs. This requires creating an indigenous framework within which your product line can be displayed. Assume, for example, that a U.S. firm decides South African tourism offers markets for its product line of processed snacks. It resolves to establish product outlets in KwaZulu-Natal, adjacent to some or all of the 152 wild game reserves, game ranches, wetland parks, nature reserves, forest reserves, hunting reserves, and crocodile farms—all wildlife destinations in that province (Pooley and Player 1995).

The plan poses problems. First, provincial law forbids commercial outlets in wilderness areas; sites must be located just outside them. However, placing tourist-oriented shops within nearby African communities may create enmity if their members see no benefit for themselves. Nowadays, rural Africans actively resent what they perceive as "white" commercial establishments in which European staff cater to European clientele while their African neighbors neither earn money nor learn skills. I know one private game ranch that employs *only* African neighbors, while a nearby coastal resort uses ten-foot electric fences to keep *its* African neighbors out. Each rural community reacts accordingly. The first group protects its white neighbors, perceiving the game ranch as part of its own community. The second group, excluded from the resort, steals from it.

It may not be enough, however, to just employ local workers. Indeed, to do so may compound your problems with rural neighbors. Labor-management relations are intensely adversarial throughout South Africa and may create continuous conflict. In the long run, it may well be wiser to adopt and sponsor a whole community, so that they adopt and sponsor you.

The Umfolozi Rhino Boys

As an illustration, let us explore the problems an imaginary firm would face in establishing a single outlet near KwaZulu's Umfolozi Game Reserve, world famous for its rhino. The reserve has a solid economic future, but one that excludes Zulu subsistence farming families who live near it. Some families attempt to supplement their income by carving wooden rhino for their sons to sell to Western tourists who pass through to view the game. However, sales are rare. The carvings are identical; each boy stands alone, on one side of a dust-filled road, ten yards from his neighbor. Together, they form a one-mile line of ragged, dusty sellers.

Each boy holds up two rhino, mutely offering them for sale. Tourists, intent on reaching the reserve after hours on the roads, race by at sixty miles an hour—pursued by clouds of rolling dust, which then engulf the boys. To draw attention, the boys leap, shout, whistle, and finally curse the drivers for not stopping, even throwing rocks to make their point. In the rainy season, the roads flood, tourists stay home, and sales drop to zero.

Assume an adviser from this imaginary firm meets first with family elders to ask if he might work with their sons (carvers) and grandsons (sellers) to help both groups earn more. Gaining permission, he might initially advise each carving family to expand and modify their product line, sharply differentiating the carvings (as they once did, before the advent of mass tourism), with each carver developing a recognizable style.

He could then recommend restructuring their market site, clustering the sellers by transforming their single line into two adjacent market squares (one on each side of the road), to draw both arriving and returning traffic. The expanded product line would also be clustered, but only in one section of each square. To provide roles for women and girls, he might advise that tourists would be more attracted by drums and dancing than by boys whistling and throwing rocks. He could then fill a second section of each market square with drums and weaving lines of chanting dancers.

The adviser might further diversify the local product line, suggesting the families move beyond carving to also providing those goods and services that people really want after hours spent on rural roads. Since Umfolozi is four hours from a major city, with no roadside restaurants en route, travelers might well stop for (the firm's) processed foods, soft drinks, or tea and coffee. Although the roadside coffee concept barely exists in rural South Africa, bored and weary drivers would at least slow down and look, especially if forewarned by several hand-made signs. Since snacks, drinks, carvings, drums, and dances would be clustered in each market square, the atmosphere would be inviting. When tourists stop to eat, drink, then watch (or join) the dancing, they are also more likely to buy carvings.

Next, integrate additional segments of the sponsor's product line into the display. This step can require further training. Processed foods and drinks could be marketed as single-item take-aways, or opened, prepared, and more artfully displayed in (locally woven) "safari picnic baskets." Adjacent picnic sites with toilets could be established, particularly in regions where wildlife will roam through them and act as cleanup crews. Hot meals (again incorporating segments of the product line) could be prepared to Western tastes as sit-down lunches and dinners. Moving beyond food, safari caps, clothing, and equipment could be offered. There are, in fact, few limits to the services that both sponsors and their clients could provide.

———

Rural sponsorship is an unconventional way to enter peasant markets. Admittedly, it may seem quicker, easier, and cheaper to drive up to village stores and unload goods. There are advantages, however, in working with rural communities rather than around them.

First, your sponsorship can be an on-site training course in rural market entry. Foreign managers (or their staff) who merely drop off goods learn too little about their buyers, gaining no insight into which directions to expand. In contrast, sponsorship provides your personnel with on-site language training, rural field experience, new connections, and, ultimately, insight into further market penetration.

Most important, sponsorship can be a form of business life insurance. As mentioned earlier, each group you sponsor will sponsor you. They may defend you against other factions who might perceive your venture as exploitation rather than straightforward commerce. You may, in short, be favorably received, acquiring a reputation for both benevolence and business. That can be useful. In South Africa's explosive atmosphere, a foreign firm will find that developing people as well as profits will enhance both its social acceptance and its political survival.

References

Beckett, Jamie. 1990. "Asia: The Must Have Market of the 1990s." *San Jose Mercury* (December).

Bornstein, David. 1995. "The Barefoot Bank with Cheek." *Atlantic Monthly* (December), 40–47.

Creekmore, Charles. 1986. "Misunderstanding Africa." *Psychology Today* (December), 41–46.

Cunningham, Anthony. 1991. "The Herbal Medicine Trade: Resource Depletion and Environmental Management for a 'Hidden Economy'." In *South Africa's Informal Economy*, edited by E. Preston-Whyte and C. Rogerson, 196–98. Cape Town: Oxford University Press.

Dahle, Cheryl. 1999. "Industry that Can Improve Peoples' Lives." *Fast Company* (April), 167–76.

Dixon, Craig. 1999. Staff member of the firm Trickle Up. Personal conversation (July).

Fadiman, Jeffrey. 1994. "Tapping Third World Peasant Markets." *What Can Multinationals Do for Peasants?*, edited by H. Serrie and S. Burkhalter, 53–84. Studies in Third-World Societies, no. 49, College of William and Mary. Aspects of this chapter are adapted from this publication with Dr. Serrie's permission.

James, Barry. 1998. "A Winning Policy: Lend to the Poor." *International Herald Tribune* (7 March).

Janis, Pam. 1997. "Broken Down and Abandoned on the Information Highway." *International Herald Tribune* (4 August).

Kammen, Daniel. 1995. "Cookstoves for the Developing World." *Scientific American* (July), 72–75.

Kraft, S. 1987. "Africa's Tiny Shops Thrive amid Poverty." *Los Angeles Times* (24 March).

Mathews, Jessica. 1993. "A Success in Helping the Poor." *International Herald Tribune* (21 December).

Millman, Joel. 1991. "The Merchant of Mexico." *Forbes* (5 August), 80.

Mnyanda, Lukanyo. 1996. "Afrika Bakery Hits the High Road." *Enterprise* (November), 82.

Naidoo, Yasantha. 1995. "My Hat." *Sunday Tribune,* Natal (2 April); also discussions with Jenny Kirkland, Obanjeni founder, August 1996.

Pooley, Tony, and Ian Player. 1995. *KwaZulu-Natal Wildlife Destinations*. Cape Town: Southern Book Publishers.

Serrie, Hendrick. 1994. "Peasants as Customers of Multinational Firms." *What Can Multinationals Do for Peasants?*, edited by H. Serrie and S. Burkhalter, 13–14. Studies in Third-World Societies, no. 49, College of William and Mary.

Trade Union Research Project (TURP). 1994. *A User's Guide to the South African Economy*. Durban: Y Press, 64.

Van der Walt, Terry. 1996. "In Just 7 Days…I can make you a home." *Sunday Tribune,* Natal (16 June).

Warren, William. 1983. *Jim Thompson: The Legendary American of Thailand*. Bangkok: Jim Thompson Thai Silk Company, 56–74.

Yunis, Mohammed. CEO, Grameen (Countryside) Bank, Bangladesh. 1997. Radio broadcast, "All Things Considered," KQED, San Francisco, May.

8

Urban Marketing:
Analyze the Townships

There are several ways to market in South
Africa's black townships. Unfortunately, none of
them are European. Forget every white rule you
know. Just sit and watch and try to comprehend
their rules of play. After awhile, you see that
you've been playing rugby and they've been
playing cricket. You try to be a bit more African
yourself and suddenly you're much easier for
them to deal with. Then, you might consider
township marketing.

—Anthony G. Cadman

Having analyzed the rural markets, you should next examine
South Africa's townships. They have evolved dramatically since
The Turn in 1994. Not only has the potential clientele expanded,
but the very concept of urban marketing has acquired an additional
dimension. You will recall that marketers in the apartheid era
focused solely on what were then all-white cities. They
now compete to penetrate the far more massive all-black townships.
Today's maps of Johannesburg display central Soweto
as an extension of its business district, where earlier ones either
ignored it or placed it outside the urban zone.

Government policy now calls for the creation of commercial
corridors to link all townships with their respective urban
cores. To carry out this policy the townships must receive suffi-

cient water, electricity, sewerage, and transport, to permit the creation of genuine urban infrastructures. Each township core, as mentioned earlier, will also acquire meeting, shopping, and recreational outlets, all meant to turn these once-stagnant dormitory communities into vibrant urban magnets, explicitly intended to generate commerce. One reason to examine townships, therefore, is that they are now alive with commercial potential.

A second reason to investigate these areas is to discover empty niches. White firms shunned township ventures until Mandela's presidency. They were not only deterred by black political militancy but also by the belief that African income was too low to justify investment. As a result, the modern retail outlets that we associate with urban shopping avoided these locations.

Today, both fears have diminished. Township militancy is declining. African spending may rise over the next decade to R278 billion—as compared to R190 billion by Whites (Morris 1992a). Experts also note that thousands of younger township Blacks have shed their tribal identities, redefining themselves as *towni* (townsfolk) and speaking towni dialects rather than tribal languages. In brief, millions of once-oppressed township citizens seem poised to become modern consumers. Those empty retail niches can now be filled.

One final reason to analyze the township market is to learn how other firms have fared. First, consider a large firm. Standard Bank installed automatic teller machines in Khayelitsha, an impoverished Xhosa township near Cape Town. Each office branch is a small storefront with glass doors always open, thus avoiding the image of bank tellers behind bars that Africans can find intimidating. Customers who wait in line relax with Xhosa music. Xhosa clerks guide first-time clients through ATM procedures, using local dialect. Depositors receive interest on their savings, higher status (a street address), service (financial advice), and safety (a stop card, if their ATM card is stolen). More important, they are provided with an unconventional solution to a township problem: robbery on payday.

> Before opening her first [ATM] account, Ms.
> Mvunyiswa had been robbed numerous times by
> knife-toting tsotsis, often en route to deliver
> money to her relatives. Now she deposits her
> wages in ATMs that can also be accessed by her
> kinfolk…far away. (Wells 1996, 1)

Compare Standard Bank's experience with that of a small firm, Bimbo's Fast Foods. In white areas, it offers American-style fast foods, served in a clean, safe environment. When Bimbo's moved to the townships, however, it transformed itself into The Africa Hut. The menu changed to African staples, served with quality ingredients and at low prices. Like Standard Bank, The Africa Hut offered service (short waiting times), status (clean, upscale settings), and safety (well lighted, with security guards). More important, it, too, provided an unconventional solution to a township problem: finding traditional food in modern, urban settings. The success of both large and small enterprises suggests that other entrepreneurs who blend service, safety, status, and new solutions into their product lines can meet widespread needs.

Township Analysis

Street Survey

Begin your township analysis by surveying the streets. Walk and ride with your research team to compile a street-by-street survey so extensive as to let you create your own map, rather than relying on any other. Chart streets, paths, landmarks, and the time it takes to move between them. Government maps may be inaccurate, outdated, and incomplete, depicting main roads but ignoring secondary routes and smaller paths. Commercial township maps have yet to be developed—thus suggesting still another market niche.

This first survey should accomplish three objectives. The least important is just to learn your way (in daylight and darkness) around irregular and confusing road networks, devoid of street signs. The second is to learn how much time it takes to reach main points along these routes, so as to schedule future segments of your project with increasing accuracy. These times may vary seasonally, since rains can flood the routes. Consequently, if you plan to work within fixed schedules, make contingency plans ahead of time.

The final problem is to learn which routes are safe. Remember that crime dominates parts of every township, and carjacking, robbery, burglary, and assault pose genuine threats. This third objective, therefore, is to identify the routes along which crimes occur and then avoid them. In Soweto, for example, carjackers tend to work certain areas in daylight, others at night. In KwaMashu township (Durban), factional feuds render certain routes unsafe for outsiders. Others are safe for everyone. Local residents know which they are. Ask them.

Talk with both taxi drivers and their clientele. Townships are commuter communities, filled with people who spend hours chatting while awaiting public transport. They will gladly chat with you. Taximen stay up-to-date by talking with their riders. Both groups may be valuable informants. I learned this on my first day in KwaZulu, when a taxi driver drove two hours to my new home. He talked throughout the trip about his township, at that time locked into a miniwar between political parties. He taught me more of township lore than I could ever have learned inside a library. Then, he offered to drive me into those neighborhoods where he could guarantee a welcome and thus ensure my safety. In short, he launched my research.

One word of caution: some taxis are unsafe. The industry has grown to over one hundred thousand vehicles, primarily sixteen-seat minibuses, formed into Black Taxi Associations (BTAs). Some BTAs have turned on one another, attacking the cars, drivers, and clients of competitors. All sides have called on tsotsi gangs for protection, some of whom have taken over the associations they protect (Bank 1991). In some areas, sporadic taxi wars take place, often with semiautomatic weapons.

> The streets of Kranskop resembled the "Wild
> West" yesterday…as rival factions in a taxi war
> produced AK-47 rifles and, hanging out of their
> vehicles, fired wildly at each other….
> (Oellermann 1997)

Learn which groups fight, as well as why, how, when, and where.

Neighborhood Analysis: Tribe and Class

Explore the neighborhoods from your own commercial perspective. Every township can be segmented into neighborhoods, often marked by sharp divisions. You will initially discover that the oldest ones are tribal, in that residents came from one tribal homeland, speak its language, and follow its customs. This is due to apartheid. Until the 1950s ethnolinguistic zoning (segregation by tribe) was imposed on every township. Remember that by segregating urban workers, the government hoped to minimize factional fighting and maximize control. In Gauteng's Daveyton Township, for example, long, narrow strips of land were originally assigned to Sotho, Zulu, or Swazi workers. They have now become long, narrow Sotho-, Zulu-, or Swazi-speaking neighborhoods (Pirie 1984). The same pattern occurs elsewhere.

In contrast, you will find newer neighborhoods that define themselves by social class. Some of these emerged when apartheid-era authorities housed workers from several tribal groups together, forcing them to generate a multitribal culture. Most, however, simply settled in groups that reflected their members' economic status, regardless of tribe. Outsiders often view entire townships as one-class shanty towns, populated solely by the poor. In fact, many neighborhoods display a complex, class-based social structure. In Soweto, for example, four million citizens have formed distinct neighborhoods that reflect at least seven social classes, groupings that exist in most other townships as well.

Luxury Neighborhoods. These neighborhoods contain the Sowetan mega-elite. They emerged in the 1970s when a multi-national corporation constructed upper-middle-class housing for its employees in a part of Soweto now known as "Beverly Hills." This group was joined by members of the political elite (among them, Winifred Madikizela-Mandela) and thereafter by newly affluent businessmen, all of whom built increasingly elaborate homes. Mega-elitists also appear in other urbanized townships. Together, they constitute a small but expanding luxury market, oriented (as African tradition dictates) toward conspicuous consumption and display (Dia 1991).

Upper-Middle-Class Neighborhoods. These areas house an older, less affluent, multitribal elite, which we might call the "professionals." This group emerged in the 1940s among African lawyers, doctors, clergy, teachers, and a few retailers. In Johannesburg, this group was allotted a specified suburb in Soweto, a pattern then followed in other townships. This is a conservative clientele, more oriented toward efficient services than luxury goods, and concerned with status and appearances rather than consumption and display.

Middle-Class Neighborhoods. Originally formed by a younger elite, these neighborhoods might be called "company towns." They were constructed after the 1976 Soweto riots, which convinced foreign and South African corporations of the need for African housing. Consequently, several firms con-structed substantial numbers of identical, middle-class homes for junior management staff, initially in Soweto and then else-where. The original homeowners were joined by other mem-bers of what is now considered the black middle class, many of whom remodeled or expanded the original housing to the point where the earlier architectural similarities have disap-peared (Parnell and Mather 1990). In other townships such as Kagiso, near Johannesburg, middle-class housing has emerged along its outer rim (Keller 1993). This is a display-oriented clientele, interested in clothing, cars, TV, sports, and music.

Working-Class ("Matchbox") Neighborhoods. "Matchbox" neighborhoods dominate every township. They were originally built for migrant workers, who were each assigned one among thousands of tiny, three- or four-room houses, derisively labeled by critics as matchboxes. These were identical, inside and out, and were constructed row on row (on sand flats or dusty tableland) to the point where they suggested the monotony of cornfields. Since occupants could only rent, homes were never improved, and the unceasing influx of new job seekers led to subletting and overcrowding. Nonetheless, over time many of these migrants found jobs, began families, and improved their homes. As a result, many matchbox owners now aspire to middle-class status, a wish reflected in both the tidiness of their homes and an interest in safe, familiar (Western) brand names.

Migrant Worker (Hostel) Neighborhoods. Composed solely of barracklike hostels, these neighborhoods house the marginally employed in every urban township. There are several hundred thousand hostel dwellers in South Africa, who live in barracks operated by the mines, municipalities, or churches. Most hostels are tribalized, drawing people from one homeland. As noted earlier, where tribes embrace opposing political parties, hostel dwellers wage war with semiautomatic weapons (Pirie and da Silva 1986). In Johannesburg, for instance, Zulu and Xhosa hostel dwellers launch what are actually tribal attacks in the names of Inkatha Freedom Party and Mandela's African National Congress.

Hostel life is shabby and bleak. Some barracks have light but no heat, forcing residents to endure winters so cold their drinking water freezes. Some men work at subsistence wages; some peddle licit and illicit goods and services to other residents: snuff, beer, drugs, stolen goods, laundry, shoe repair, sex, and gambling. As a result, this population is socially isolated from other township neighborhoods. Even the matchbox residents view hostel dwellers with distrust and disdain: "We can't have on our doorstep a cage with people who live in herds, who don't live with women…and have a beer yard for their nightly entertainment" (Pirie and da Silva).

This isolation can also be enforced. Some hostels are fenced, with entry and exit by a single, guarded gate. Some seal off each subsection with steel doors to prevent internal rioting. Nonetheless, the hostel dwellers are not prisoners, but potential clientele. They work, earn, and wish to buy. No marketer should ignore them.

Squatter Neighborhoods. Encircling every township are squatter neighborhoods that house an under-/unemployed class now estimated at eight million (Scholand 1996). They are the product of an Africa-wide urban migration, in which the image of city life has become a magnet that attracts both the desperate and the bold. They arrive seeking mates, work, adventure, and hope; they find prostitution, joblessness, boredom, and despair. They live in huts of tin, tar paper, cardboard, and gunnysacks that expose them to heat, dust, rain, and cold. They cook with wood, kerosene, or coal, often in open oil drums that expose them to sulphur dioxide, nitrogen oxide, and soot. It is a way of life that gradually destroys the only thing they have to offer—their health.

Nonetheless, no marketer should ignore the squatter segment. They may lack formal employment, yet all of them work at something and everyone wants to work more. They form the core of South Africa's black (informal) market, working in a system based both on cash and barter. Collectively, they handle vast sums of money. An estimated \$3–\$5 million changes hands every day, just in Soweto (Wells). Do not ignore them, either as colleagues or consumers. In fact, they form an irregular army of street-savvy buyers and sellers, who follow township trends and can teach you township marketing from new perspectives.

Tsotsi Neighborhoods. These form tiny pockets in the squatter community. Remember that the tsotsi make up the townships' gangster class. These people also work; they are fully employed as predators in every township. Some gangs are sophisticated, multitribal operations, headquartered overseas. Most are clan or tribal bands that specialize in specific crimes, whether cat burglary, commuter assault, train robbery, or carjacking. Other gangs may be only factional fighters, breaking the boredom of unemployment by getting drunk and doing battle on the weekends. Your task, at this stage, is to identify, locate, and learn enough about them to find out which, if any, you can work with.

Infrastructure Analysis

Examine the commercial infrastructure that forms the heart of every township. If that heart is healthy, it will be filled with active shops and busy people. You will find, however, that most township cores are hollow. They lack the restaurants, nightclubs, parks, and other gathering points that draw people who bring them to life. Today, most of these centers consist of semi-occupied buildings, dusty streets, and idle people passing time. Under apartheid, white officials prohibited development of township centers. Townships were to be inhabited by male transients; they had no cores. They were built to warehouse people and transport them back and forth to work. Today's townships are in transition. Soweto has considerable infrastructure, whereas more rural townships have none at all. Nonetheless, each remains hollow to the degree that it fails to meet local needs. Government promises of help may also prove hollow, in which case private firms must fill the void.

Analyze public transport, which forms the infrastructure of every township. Those near Cape Town and Johannesburg are serviced by a railway that runs into each city's center. Others are served by buses and minivans. Urban townships also have more expensive sedan taxis. Viewed as a whole, however, the transit systems are incomplete. They still move people in and out of the city rather than throughout the neighborhoods in such fashion as to integrate them into a coherent whole. Public transit is also overcrowded and invariably late. Buses and taxis move only when completely filled, making schedules impossible. In consequence, too much of each commuter's day is spent standing and waiting for transport to arrive. To learn about this market segment, locate where they wait, then stand with them and talk.

Examine the electric power structure. It should form the arteries of every township, providing heat and light. Government spokesmen declare that 63 percent of African homes are electrified (*Los Angeles Times* 1999). This still leaves thousands upon thousands unserved—both in the countryside and in townships. Nonetheless, this unserved market segment does have access to electricity. Ask township residents, therefore, as to the extent of both official and illicit power grids.

The illicit electricity networks can be found in every township near existing official power sources. They are created by teenage "voltage bandits." These young entrepreneurs tap into the official grid, then string new lines into tiny, handmade electrical substations. From there they run them into huts and squatter shacks to power lights, refrigerators, and TVs. Residents pay the boys for initial installation and subsequent repairs. In Kagiso Township, for example, teenagers have wired an estimated 90 percent of the five thousand squatter shacks on its impoverished rim (Keller).

Financial Analysis

Look once more at the townships' financial infrastructure, particularly the stokvels. You will recall that research on rotating funds across Africa suggests that borrowers from Western banks default more often and that repayment to rotating funds runs near 98 percent. One World Bank official argues that this higher repayment rate validates the value of (traditional) ritual as a financial guarantee (Dia). Clearly, this type of fund is both African and successful.

Pay particular attention to the most sophisticated of these enterprises. The wealthiest township stokvels, having endured for decades, are now bankrolled by African elites and are called High Budget Revolving Credit Associations. Their names are listed in the newspaper *Sowetan* on Fridays. Socially, they follow African models, restricting membership to people who are linked to one another. Commercially, they have adopted Western business methods, including governing boards, modern offices, formal correspondence, and Western bookkeeping.

They pay out only a percentage of the funds collected, in order to invest the balance. They also make loans (on request, rather than in rotation) at rates below those of township *amashonisa* (loan sharks), which can reach 100 percent per week. Meeting their officers could prove mutually beneficial, as they seek investment opportunities, keep their fingers on each township's economic pulse, and may find reasons to cooperate with you. For an outsider such as yourself, they offer previously unexplored sources of capital, credit, connections, and consulting, along with a window into township trends no Western bank can match.

Consumer Analysis

Spending Patterns

The township youth population is exploding. Thirty-nine percent of African urbanites are now said to be under fourteen. Some are unemployed; most leave school to work but are underemployed; many peddle; still others hustle or work with gangs. From a marketer's perspective, this makes all of them "stay-at-homes"; they spend both days and nights within the townships. In contrast, older residents leave to work each day. Whatever township money is spent on weekdays must come from the young (Morris 1992a). This group seeks products that promote pleasure, entertainment, excitement, risk, youthful status, and personal appearance (Elliot 1998).

You will also discover that the women do all food and household shopping. In townships, shopping is not perceived as pleasant; it is hard, physical work. The shopping commute can be long and tiring, particularly when the ability to carry heavy purchases is limited. South African shopping outlets often follow European shopping hours, thereby eliminating evenings, Saturday afternoons, and Sundays as shopping times. The average township woman spends 41 percent of her income on food (Morris 1992a). With such limited funds, she can make no mistakes. She is a conservative shopper who seeks safety in reliable brands and reliable sellers.

Men shop sporadically, usually for leisure items that can range from cars to clothing, music, cigarettes, and beer. Many label every store they patronize by color, perceiving them as Black or White according to the image each projects. White stores copy Western models, offering clean, well-lighted interiors, low noise levels, formal product display, high (fixed) prices, and inflexible (or no) credit policies. They attract older, middle-aged, and middle- and upper-class black clientele.

Black stores follow African models, offering staff informality, higher noise levels, informal product display, African music, flexible pricing, and accessible credit. These attract younger, single, blue-collar (or marginally employed) African customers, who patronize outlets where they feel accepted, prices are lower, and credit is offered on terms they understand (Imerman 1985).

Sales Outlets: Spaza Shops

Analyze the distribution chains related to your field. Begin by contacting township administrators for the permissions needed to conduct township research. Next, seek introductions to selected wholesalers who can pass you on to favored retailers. Visiting each link within these distribution chains may provide unexpected insights. Tracing the distribution of Portuguese (sugared) bread, for example, leads you from bakeries to wholesalers and from there to self-service supermarkets, counter-service markets, tuck (cake and candy) shops, petrol stations, mobile snack canteens, and, finally, to the backs of pickup trucks and folding tables on the street.

Then locate the "spaza shops," a South African township tradition. They can be found near the bottom of every chain of distribution, and each neighborhood has more than one. They are what pioneer Americans once called general stores, meeting places where neighbors gathered to gossip—and they will gossip with you. *Spaza*, however, is township slang for "not real" (invisible). In fact, the word means "stores that are not really stores."

The term comes from the apartheid era, when Bantu retailing was illegal. Spazas therefore operated from private homes (and squatter shacks) without licenses, advertising, product display, or any other overt sign of being shops (Morris 1987). They were legalized in 1989, but owners still fear to draw attention. Many remain invisible, thus avoiding visits from either the authorities or tsotsis. Most open when schools close as well as any other time clients drop by. They thrive on word of mouth, which is first spread by children to their families. Adults visit what is after all a private home and leave with basic goods. In this way, the spazas acquire lifetime clientele.

Spazas are basic. Some set up shop in empty packing cases, gleaned from foreign firms (Rissik 1994). Others operate from one room in a shack. More work out of backyards, securing stock through teenage runners who carry the goods on foot from wholesalers. The owners then store them in their kitchens and bedrooms each night (Rogerson 1991).

You may initially dismiss the spazas as economically insignificant and thus not worth analysis. This is unwise; many have become commercially important, generating thousands of Rand per year without altering their external appearance. By 1990, over sixty-six thousand spazas were estimated as generating an annual turnover of three to seven billion Rand (Rogerson). More important, spaza owners and clientele know more about their neighborhoods than do modern outlet owners, most of whom commute from distant suburbs. Nor should spazas be overlooked as marketing outlets. *Drum Magazine*, a major South African publication, now markets through a network of over 5,000 spazas in Gauteng alone (Morris 1992b). It has blazed a useful trail for outsiders.

Leisure Meeting Places: *Shebeens*

Every neighborhood supports one or more *shebeens*. A shebeen is a drinking place, usually operated by a woman known as a "shebeen queen." The original word (from Gaelic) means "little dram shop," which in turn suggests the unlicensed (illegal) sale of alcoholic spirits (de Haas 1991). Shebeens were originally developed by rural women who had moved to the city and could produce the sorghum beer enjoyed by men of every tribe. Although shebeens were illegal under apartheid, they operated as invisibly and effectively as spazas.

Over time, some of the original backyard-and-kitchen shebeens evolved into more sophisticated establishments, reflecting the increasingly complex social structure of their respective townships. This change proved useful to township consumers, many of whom patronize the shebeens to display what they perceive as class distinctions. Specific groups band together to create a distinctive public image, then display that image in their clothes, music, dancing, and what they drink. In consequence, since several types of shebeen have appeared in every township, visiting each type will introduce you to a different social class. In KwaZulu, for example, one researcher (de Haas) suggests you should visit the following: regular shebeens, spots, taverns, and licensed bars.

Regular shebeens serve a tribal clientele: young, recent migrants from rural areas, elderly working men, and the marginally employed of every age. They offer sorghum beer, either home brewed or factory produced. Conversation and music are Zulu.

Spots (or Spotti) mainly serve the *amapansula* (cool dressers), the youthful, towni marginal workers with little education, who may work independently but illicitly, operating just beyond the fringes of tsotsi gangs. They dress "high" (expensively), favoring Pierre Cardin shirts and Florsheim shoes. They speak "Tsotsi Taal," share distinctive music, and dance their own dances. Spots provide this status-oriented clientele with "Whiteman's (malt) beer."

Taverns may or may not be licensed by municipal authorities, and they serve two types of prestige-oriented, urban clientele: "dudes" and "cats." Male dudes dress in narrow trousers, high-heeled shoes, and pastel shirts. They have permed hair and one earring. Male cats dress in black with pointed shoes. Both groups are usually married high school graduates with clerical jobs; they dance to American music (blues, jazz), speak English with American slang, and drink U.S. and European beers.

Licensed bars draw Westernized elites: middle-aged and older, married white-collar professionals. They dress in Western style, speak formal (anglicized) English, and drink expensive wines, beers, and harder liquors from South Africa, the United States, and Europe.

This model is oversimplified. In reality some shebeen queens offer dual or even multilevel service, providing malt beer to "notables" in the owner's home, for instance, and offering home-brewed sorghum beer to the "ordinaries" in her backyard. Similarly, licensed bars may send drinkers into separate rooms, with elitists drinking whiskey in one while middle-class customers order malt beer in another. In short, shebeens reflect the social position of their clientele.

Shebeens may prove useful as potential marketing outlets, for both low- and high-end products. One Sotho agricultural cooperative, for instance, recently collected more tomatoes than it could sell. After exhausting the traditional outlets (schools, hospitals, etc.), it brewed what remained into tomato beer, selling it to area shebeens. This low-end concept proved so profitable the group has turned to full-time brewing (Philip 1993).

Similarly, one high-end firm entered township markets by marketing "Clubman Mint Punch" through shebeens. The product catered to a township tradition: drinking alcohol at lunch. If employers disapprove, workers eat mints to dispel the scent before returning to work. The punch mixed alcohol and mint, thus allowing purchasers to avoid alcoholic odors, evade censure, and save the cost of mints (Morris 1992a). Both cases suggest that shebeen owners seem open to commercial innovation and may see innovative ways to work with you.

On-Site Analysis: Do It Yourself

Hands-on analysis will prove of greatest value if you do much of it yourself. Only by personally collecting township data can you come to understand the township markets, in part because they change so rapidly, but also because you learn most when you see the markets through African eyes. In short, one of your goals should be to spend time in the townships. Do more than just survey; explore, connect, converse. In time, you will intuitively sense what they are about, where their future lies, and why. Then, you might consider township marketing.

References

Bank, Leslie. 1991. "A Culture of Violence: The Migrant Taxi Trade in Qwa-Qwa, 1980–1990." In *South Africa's Informal Economy*, edited by E. Preston-Whyte and C. Rogerson, 124–41. Cape Town: Oxford University Press. Bank's analysis of Qwa-Qwa is equally valid elsewhere.

Cadman, Anthony G. Chairman, Anthony Cadman Associates, South Africa. 1996. Personal conversations.

de Haas, Mary. 1991. "Of Joints and Jollers: Culture and Class in Natal Shebeens." In *South Africa's Informal Economy*, edited by E. Preston-Whyte and C. Rogerson, 101–13. Cape Town: Oxford University Press.

Dia, Mamadou. 1991. "Development and Cultural Values in Sub-Saharan Africa." *Finance Development*. International Monetary Fund and World Bank (December): 11.

Elliot, Stuart. 1998. "Global Consumers: Birds of a Feather." *International Herald Tribune* (26 June), 15, 19.

Imerman, Ilana. 1985. "Store Selection amongst Black Consumers." M.A. thesis, University of the Witwatersrand, Johannesburg, 36–38, 70ff, 100ff.

Keller, Bill. 1993. "South Africa's Voltage Pirates." *San Francisco Chronicle* (12 September).

Los Angeles Times. 1999 (26 May).

Menaker, Drusilla. 1995. "Soweto, South Africa: Brisk Business in the Townships." *Business Week* (25 September), 125.

Morris, Robin. 1992a. *Marketing to Black Townships: Practical Guidelines.* Cape Town: Juta & Co., 63–105. I consider Morris South Africa's leading authority on township marketing. He is managing director of Dynamics Advertising, Durban.

Morris, Robin, ed. 1992b. "Drum and True Love in the Spazas." *Black Market Report* 7, no 22, Durban, Damelin Education Group (17 August): 7.

———, ed. 1987. "The Sphaza [sic] Shop—The Shop that Is Not a Shop." *Black Market Report* 2, no 8, Durban, Damelin Education Group (19 June): 22.

Oellermann, Ingrid. 1997. "Kranskop Turns Into 'Wild West' as Taxi Rivals Go on the Rampage." *Natal Mercury* (11 February).

Parnell, Susan, and Charles Mather. 1990. "Upgrading the Matchboxes: Urban Renewal in Soweto, 1976–86." In *Economic Growth and Urbanization in Developing Areas,* edited by D. Drakakis-Smith, 238–49. London: Routledge.

Philip, Kate. 1993. "Towards Democratic Management in Coops." In *African Management: Philosophies, Concepts and Applications*, edited by L. Mbigi, P. Christie, and R. Lessem, 269–76. Randburg, South Africa: Knowledge Resources.

Pirie, G. H. 1984. "Ethno-Linguistic Zoning in South African Black Townships." *Area* 16, no. 4: 291–98.

Pirie G. H., and M. da Silva. 1986. "Hostels for African Migrants in Greater Johannesburg." *GeoJournal* 12, no. 2: 173–82.

Rissik, Dee. 1994. *Culture Shock: South Africa*. Portland, OR: Graphic Arts Center Publishing, 227–28.

Rogerson, Christian. 1991. "Home-Based Enterprises of the Urban Poor: The Case of Spazas." In *South Africa's Informal Economy*, edited by E. Preston-Whyte and C. Rogerson, 336–43. Cape Town: Oxford University Press.

Scholand, Michael. 1996. "Re-Energizing South Africa." *World Watch* (September-October), 24.

Wells, Ken. 1996. "Money Machines: Its New ATMs in Place, a Bank Reaches out to South Africa's Poor." *Wall Street Journal* (13 June), 1, 9.

9

Urban Strategy: Market through Black Marketers

I seethe at street peddlers in the U.S., who pay no taxes, no rent, no employee withholding or self-employment tax. They are leeches on the American Economy.

—Daniel M. Evans

Uncontrolled hawking was considered by planners of urban South Africa to be an undesirable activity...unsightly and often economically marginal street traders, peddling their wares on pavements...were seen by municipal officials to be the antithesis of economic development.

—Timothy Mosdell

For observers surrounded by glass and concrete it requires a leap of the imagination to perceive the informal sector as a thriving economic activity and source of future wealth.

—Maritz van Zyl

Black Marketing Has an Image Problem

To fully understand South Africa's urban market, you must research its "shadow" (black market) economy. South African cities and townships have one common characteristic. The overwhelming majority of their African population must buy and sell within the black market to maintain their living standards. To reach them, we must do the same.

You may have little experience in marketing to this sector. Among Americans, black marketing has a serious image problem. Many see it as a shadow world, an underground refuge for illicit money changers, smugglers, and tax evaders. We perceive black marketers across the world as engaging in illegal and unethical practices. Americans believe in rules; black marketers seem to work outside them. Thus we equate this type of marketing with life outside the law.

In consequence, black market methods are not perceived of as U.S. business tools: they are never taught in U.S. business schools and are ignored in business books. Since our firms exclude these methods from their training, few American managers exploit them overseas. In South Africa, for instance, most American enterprises confine their efforts to the formal economic sector, marketing primarily to black and white elites. Too few consider the larger informal sector, where thousands of black marketers sell successfully to hundreds of thousands of clients.

Our distaste for this type of marketing is reflected in the word we have chosen over the centuries to describe it. Historically, Caucasian Americans have equated the color black with evil and apply the word to this type of commerce. European translations reflect and antedate our own: in French, *marché noir*; in German, *schwarzer Markt*; in Czech, *cerny trh*, and so on. In contrast, African terms for the same institution (Kenya, *magendo*; Congo, *matabiche*, etc.) often translate as "free market," implying the freedom to operate beyond the reach of government. Only recently have a few Americans begun to understand this sense of freedom and to use more positive terms that describe this sector as the core of an *informal, parallel, hidden, shadow, underground*, or *invisible* economy.

Many Americans also condemn black marketing exactly because it suggests freedom. Because they perceive it as unregulated, they consider it dangerous. Black market hawkers may appear anywhere and sell at any price. Owners of established outlets fear their own profits will be undercut, since hawkers without overhead can sell at lower prices. In our own history the Jewish pushcart peddlers that thronged New York City in the 1890s were described as "unlicensed hordes," an "oriental invasion" undermining the "decent people" of America (Birmingham 1984). Today, though both the peddlers and the insults have changed, the fears remain.

Governments also object to the black market. In the former USSR, for instance, jobs were allotted solely by the state, and supplementing income in the black market was legally forbidden. Under South Africa's apartheid, jobs were allotted to Bantu by the state, and supplemental self-employment was illegal. Government officials in both nations argued that these acts were unreported, unregulated, untaxed, and thus a danger to the system. Other nations have similar laws.

Most African black markets are now too big for any government to tax or regulate. They represent more than half of all economic activity on the continent. Nigeria's black market equals 53 percent of GDP (Rupert 1998). In Zimbabwe, Lesotho, and Swaziland it approaches 60 percent (Ayers 1996); in Uganda, 66 percent (Schissel 1989); and in Sierra Leone, 87 percent (Goldberg 1997). In Somalia and Liberia, the black market has replaced the formal economy completely.

Nor can African governments regulate the multinational black market. Which government, for example, can effectively regulate West Africa's Alhazai family, whose clans move oil illegally between Niger and Nigeria, exchanging it for European luxuries? They avoid regulations, duties, and taxes by exchanging gifts and favors with kinsmen in both countries. In 1990 seventy-five Alhazai clan heads each earned nearly one million U.S. dollars per year (Parker 1994). Their power far exceeds that of the national police forces currently arrayed against them.

South Africa's black market is also too large to regulate. Figures from the most recent census (1996) show unemployment among black women at 52 percent and at 34 percent for black men (*USA Today* 1999). Thus, almost half of the population must "market black" to survive. In addition, 20 percent of those who do find work must supplement their insufficient incomes through informal market channels, as must 60 percent of the so-called working peasantry. That places tens of millions in the informal sector. While government officials might consider this too large a market segment to control, we should consider it too large a segment to ignore. This is particularly true when black marketers now handle 33 percent of all Bantu disposable income, an estimated R9.84 billion per year (Morris 1992).

How Black Markets Work

South Africa's black markets spring up everywhere. Some are permanent, such as the Umgababa markets south of Durban. Some appear and vanish, such as the tiny weekend market near KwaZulu's Richards Bay. Some string out on major roads in long, uneven lines composed of hawkers selling identical piles of nearly identical goods. Others extend like spiderwebs from bus and railway stations, tenaciously following every street and path commuters walk to reach their jobs.

Market Parameters

All of these markets are strikingly alike. Whether Sotho, Venda, or Nguni, they are based on similar traditions and operate under similar conditions. One key rule is that black markets operate via relationships, not market forces as in the West. Sellers thrive because customers buy from them regularly, thereby developing the personal bonds that ensure fair treatment and protect against deception. Since these transactions are ignored or forbidden by the government, buyers have no product guarantees and therefore no formal protection against fraud, deceptive pricing, adulteration, and so forth. They overcome these problems by establishing lifetime relationships with selected sellers, from whom they receive not only reliable products but favorable credit terms.

A second rule pertains to ease of market entry. Hawkers launch ventures with virtually no capital. Near my former KwaZulu home, for instance, one woman supports herself by harvesting and selling bite-size chunks of sugarcane. Another sews strips of antelope fur into shopping bags. A man splits, weaves, and ties bamboo into stools. Another taps his trees and sells palm wine. Such traders also have no overhead. It costs nothing to sell from a ground cloth, folding table, or wooden stall. Sales staff are family, who work without wages, while storage costs nothing if goods are stored in the traders' homes.

Two other rules pertain to unit sales and profits. Both are small. Most goods sell in units of one, whether sugarcane, mangos, or aspirin. Malaria tablets, for instance, sell at the rate of one per customer per week. Profit margins are also limited. The four sellers just mentioned earn R12–24 ($2–$4) per day. Most others earn R100 ($16–$18) per month (McIntosh 1991).

One rule appears to govern both product and price: there should be little differentiation. Most traders display identical goods in identical ways and sell, despite haggling, at near-identical prices. Indeed, sellers of similar wares cluster together to sell them, further minimizing what differences exist. I have asked cluster members how they would react if one of them sold something of higher quality at a higher or lower price. They ask why that person should compete with her sisters, since they often share the profits—so that everyone eats. Recall again that black markets run on relationships, not laws of supply and demand. The fair price is what neighbors charge. Product differentiation harms those neighbors. If we perceive the market as a pot of gold for which each trader must compete, they see it as a shallow pool of water, from which everyone sips but no one may drain.

The market parameter that governs credit terms is also based on relationships. Potential buyers regard Western forms of credit (fixed rates, fixed payment times) as cruel. They expect low rates and flexible repayment terms. Thus, the ideal client, for a black market seller, would select a product, pay part of its cost, then drop by irregularly both to chat and to pay off a bit more. Traders are most anxious to sell—and extend credit—to those with whom they either have relationships or who have been recommended by kinsfolk and friends.

Some restrictions are imposed on black market hawkers by outside forces. Since none own the land on which they sell, officials may decide at any time that the hawkers are squatters, to be expelled at whim. With no land for collateral, banks deny them loans, blocking their capacity to take root or expand. Nor can they acquire those amenities needed to make hawking either comfortable or safe. Black market sites lack water, electricity, and sanitation. They also lack protection against heat, cold, rain, dust, insects, or wild animals. Indeed, I know informal markets where the nightly cleanup is carried out solely by wild pigs and baboons.

If threatened by officials, police, mafia, or tsotsis, the hawkers have no legal recourse. If duped commercially, they cannot turn to the courts to enforce business agreements (Main 1989). Their sole defense is to form relationships with everyone with whom they deal. In summary, though able to survive, black marketers need outside help to grow.

Who "Markets Black"?

Black markets also have a human face. They overflow with people working ceaselessly to make a living. In KwaZulu's Empangeni town, for instance, a typically informal shopping mall is anchored by one formal outlet, an African-owned grocery. The sidewalks overflow with local traders shouting out the virtues of local products. Across the road, another sidewalk swarms with foreign traders, from Mozambique and Swaziland, loudly praising foreign goods. The road itself resounds with the hoots and whistles of younger hawkers, racing in between the passing cars, selling goods and services to drivers. Beyond them, local farmers sell from the backs of dusty *bakkies* (pickup trucks). Scores of radios compete to blare out music at maximum volume. The din is constant. The beat never stops. Who are these people? Who markets black?

Static Hawkers. These make up the largest group of sellers, most often older, local women who have laid permanent claim to one patch of ground in the core of each informal market. Most are widowed or divorced, with children, and they market black to survive. Since younger women are usually confined to homesteads, the old ones dominate the market. They have few formal business skills but their business intuition often leads to modest success.

A second group of static hawkers are younger—foreign men from other African nations, who cluster on the fringes of informal markets. Some five to eight million foreign Africans (estimates vary) have entered South Africa illegally since The Turn, bribing border guards; sliding under electrified fences; or evading lions, hippos, and hyenas to slip through national parks. They come from as far away as Rwanda, Nigeria, and Senegal. If police disturb them, they pay small bribes. If arrested, they pay small fines. If deported, they return.

A third, still smaller group consists of foreign women from neighboring nations, most often Swaziland and Mozambique. They are day-traders, who cross South African borders by the truckload, armed with false documents describing them as wedding guests. They alight, sell goods by their bakkies, then go back to their homelands at dusk.

Mobile Hawkers. This group, the second largest, is made up mostly of children, employed by the thousands. Girls move among the static hawkers peddling food, drink, and household goods. Boys make toys to sell to other boys. Older boys, as mentioned earlier, "run goods" between formal wholesale outlets and the static retail sales force. Others "run roads," converging on moving vehicles to sell whatever drivers will buy. Or they "run cars" as they are parked, flamboyantly directing drivers into obviously vacant spots, then offering to protect and wash their vehicles. The littlest boys may also be runners, on watch for the approach of police.

Mobile hawkers also peddle goods from door to door on weekend mornings, selling everything from sports equipment to sleeping mats. Some items are stolen, but buyers focus on their value, while sellers have the chance to make a living (Zulu 1991).

Service Providers. This is, for the most part, the wealthiest group. Black market services are usually provided by older, local men, most of whom have worked for decades in white-owned industries, thereby both saving capital and mastering the skills they now apply in black market settings. Some start their own businesses, working out of shacks along the market fringes that offer services from car repair to butchery, baking, and haircuts. Men also provide (or control) the illicit services for which no license can be obtained: gambling, prostitution, and money lending. They describe themselves as "business-men," by which they mean free-ranging entrepreneurs.

Boys also provide services. Recall the young "voltage ban-dits" who tap existing electrical grids and run wires into town-ship shacks (Keller 1993). As in adult firms, they specialize. Some (connectors) connect wires to appliances. Others (col-lectors) collect user fees. Some (steppers) simply walk the lines tracing breaks. Others (fixers) repair them. Every boy regards himself as skilled and self-employed.

Circuit Riders. Male and female circuit riders form the black marketing elite. Male and female hawkers alike yearn to own cars. Those who do use their mobility to develop distant webs of static producers and hawkers from whom they buy and who buy from them. One Zulu circuit rider drove across the northern provinces in search of trading goods. To her sur-prise, static Sotho hawkers began to buy from her, turning the buying trips into selling ventures that grew so profitable she bought a truck (Preston-Whyte 1991).

Those who graduate from static hawking to circuit riding gradually upgrade what they buy and sell. One Swazi began by traveling the "wood circuit," buying and reselling wooden combs and bowls. Then she moved into the "pot circuit," selling aluminum kitchenware. Now she offers small appliances. Such people are no longer merely hawkers but commercial innovators in constant search of new and different goods and services to offer.

Formal Outlet Owners. The owners of existing retail outlets occupy established niches in South Africa's formal economy. Some, however, are active in the informal sector as well. Often, they send buyers into the informal markets, seeking inexpensive goods for later resale in their own stores. In Swaziland, for instance, I watched the Mbabani sunrise market overflow with buyers from the biggest outlets in Johannesburg. They appeared even before sunrise and pounced on each Swazi trader as she appeared out of the night, buying the best of her products to resell at huge markups to tourists in the city.

Today, however, sourcing is more complicated, since fewer and fewer black market goods are actually produced by those who sell them. In KwaZulu, for instance, buyers from established Asian outlets come to buy "Indian" baskets, made to their order by Zulu women (Preston-Whyte), while "Zulu" baskets are now often made in India—or by white hippies from Johannesburg who copy Zulu patterns. In short, the formal and informal sectors now overlap and interact, as endless streams of trucks arrive with Indian and Chinese goods, all meant for the Zulu static hawkers to resell.

Market through the Black Marketers

No law restricts American enterprise to South Africa's formal sector. Why not work in two dimensions, marketing simultaneously to both formal and informal clientele? One simple way to reach black market buyers is by working through black market sellers. One simple way to start is to sponsor (rather than hire) the most promising among the static hawkers in a given region, transforming their current sales locations into tiny retail outlets for selected aspects of your product line.

Look for older personnel, already proven entrepreneurs, whose area knowledge and demonstrable skills can work for you. Begin by asking groups of hawkers who among them sells the most goods. They will invariably agree as to which of them is "richest." Then, ask these more successful traders who among them keeps written records of their work. Many do, especially as their business grows complex. "Rich" (female) roadside traders at KwaDlangezwa market in KwaZulu, for instance, keep records suggesting 100 percent profit on each transaction (Preston-Whyte and Nene 1991).

The next step is to learn why and how they do so well, then see if they can be of use to you. Seek innovators; black markets thrive on innovation. Zulu craftsmen will transform one hundred Coca-Cola cans into suitcases, with the logos artfully displayed for instant sale. Their Sotho counterparts snip Nestlé instant coffee cans into slivers, then artfully reshape them into candleholders. One Cape Flats trader buys a can of ice cream for R1.99, cuts it into eighty pieces, sticks a wooden sliver in each, then sells "ice cream lollies" for ten cents apiece, to make R6 daily profit (Pilot 1998). Seek out such innovators; offer to sponsor them.

Sponsoring hawkers will differ from hiring them. Launch each relationship by meeting some of their business needs, rather than merely offering wages. Are hawkers cold in winter? Provide heat. Are they hot in summer? Offer shade, drinks, and ice. Troubled by insects? Set up screening. Lack access to credit? Locate lenders. Lack legal redress? Intercede for them. Need basic math skills, bookkeeping, business English? Offer training. What better way to enter untapped markets than by doing favors that create dependence on your firm?

A second option is to sponsor hawker clans, especially where single clans monopolize specific segments of a local market. One clan may monopolize the taxi service; a second, haircutting; a third, palm wine sales. Begin by asking individual traders with whom you form relationships to introduce you to clan elders. Explore each clan's commercial needs, then selectively meet those that permit you to offer services rather than funds. Remember, your goal is not just to create relationships but also to increase dependence on those services you provide.

Such sponsorship need not be small-scale. In KwaZulu-Natal, for instance, entire clans of black market gleaners now scour the province for the bark, herbs, and roots used by *izinyanga* (herbal healers), *iziangoma* (diviners), and pharmaceutical firms to treat both real and imagined illness. Other groups gather three hundred thousand Blue Mountain Lily bulbs per year to sell in Durban (Cunningham 1991). Could an American sponsor profitably transform their operations from gleaning to managing herb and bulb farms?

A third alternative is to sponsor hawker guilds to which your preselected sellers may belong. Pietermaritzburg street traders, for instance, have formed the "Siphamandla Hawkers and Vendors Association," with over one thousand six hundred members drawn from clans in seven regions (Mosdell 1991). In Durban, the "National Nyangas' Association" and the "Herbal Traders Association" perform similar functions for that profession, with over one hundred registered formal outlets, now known as "medicine shops" (Cunningham). Similar guilds perform similar functions in Cape Town and Gauteng. In such cases, these groups function primarily as unions, offering training in negotiations with municipal authorities.

Finally, sponsor owners of selected retail outlets. They can tie you into both formal and informal channels. Within the formal sector they can retail segments of your product line to their normal clientele while simultaneously wholesaling the same items (in smaller units) to those hawkers you have also sponsored near their stores. However, selecting formal outlets in the informal market area may pose special problems. While your initial research may create the bonds you need for business interaction, there are three other criteria to consider in deciding which dealers to choose:

1. *Reputation.* How is each formal outlet owner perceived in nearby neighborhoods by formal sector competitors, in-

formal sector hawkers, and local clientele? How is the outlet itself perceived? How well could each established outlet wholesale your goods to nearby hawker outlets?

2. *Convenience.* Will each formal outlet stay open seven days/evenings a week, thereby allowing African consumers to shop at leisure? What type of credit is offered, and how is it enforced?

3. *Safety.* How safe is the immediate neighborhood in which each outlet appears. How is stock protected against what South Africans call "shrinkage" (theft), either by staff or customers, while in storage and on display? How well is the outlet itself protected against burglary after closing hours?

Remember that the answers to all three questions hinge on relationships rather than on market economics. How do members of the formal and informal sector interact? A store owner's reputation for business efficiency may not be enough to warrant sponsorship. It is more prudent to select individuals whose professional and personal reputations suggest an ability to bond with hawkers as well as clients.

Distribution in Informal Markets

Distributing goods in informal markets can create two unforeseen expenses. One is the cost of servicing large numbers of small hawker outlets. The second is the cost of protecting your goods while en route, if either criminals or civic unrest render specific neighborhoods unsafe.

One obvious option is to use your own trucks. Deliver directly to each wholesaler, then ask the hawkers you sponsor to pick up their goods there. This can both centralize and simplify your bookkeeping. As you train channel managers, periodic deliveries should become cost-effective (Morris). The disadvantage lies in the costs of buying, servicing, and protecting your fleet. Rough dirt roads that sometimes flood are hard on vehicles. Trucks with your logo may fall prey to rioters. Trucks that follow fixed routes at fixed times may be carjacked or stoned.

An alternative is to employ African delivery services. In times of unrest, mobs stone or loot those delivery vans they feel are white owned. You can minimize that risk by distributing through known and notable African families, whose reputation alone may shield your goods.

A third option is to reverse the delivery system. Ask outlet owners, hawker clan leaders, and guild officers to transport products from your headquarters to appropriate delivery points within their jurisdiction. Then hire kinsmen to protect them.

A final possibility is to distribute goods through churches. American missions, active in South Africa, have developed sophisticated distribution channels. They gather educational and religious materials at home to ship abroad for distribution in rural and urban missions. African churches do likewise, though with less reliable transport. Ally yourself with one or more churches. Ask to piggyback products into mission areas in exchange for other favors. Your firm's offer to service and repair the vehicles of an African church, for instance, may allow its ministers to safely reach worshippers in roadless, remote, or hazardous areas. In return they might offer to distribute certain of your goods en route.

Products and Packaging in Informal Markets

Packaging for the black market requires modification of both the product and the packaging. Clients are poor and want to maximize the value of each purchase. Consequently, dual-use products may prove attractive. One U.S. designer, for example, creates dual-use clothing. Each product can be converted into a carrier. She can transform a child's sweatshirt into a knapsack and back into a sweatshirt. A rain poncho can be transformed into a fanny pack when the sun shines, then back into a rain poncho as it begins to rain (Pender 1994). These creations, currently meant for wealthy segments of the American market, are based on a concept that African black market buyers would instantly accept, once modified to meet both their incomes and their needs.

To package successfully for the black market, you must transform conventional American packaging in three ways:

1. *Strengthen it.* One goal is to preserve products against Africa's climate, insects, animals, and rough handling, while simultaneously offering additional value in the packaging itself. Tins of tea, for instance, allow buyers to drink the contents and reuse the container to protect other food.

2. *Reduce it.* Package in small units. Remember, Africans buy in small quantities to cut costs and save space. Small items fit into headloads, shopping bags, bicycles, and shacks. Elaborate packaging that uses space may therefore deter purchase, as will standard American product sizes or items that are bundled together. One can of beer, for example, will sell better than either a six-pack or a bottle labeled "large economy size." The space the product takes up is more important than the lower unit price.

3. *Paint it.* African buyers value packaging as art, which you can provide by decorating your packaging so artfully that it takes on added value. Hire local artists to design local scenes and slogans for your packaging that both entertain and bring your firm to mind. These can be particularly effective if painted or stamped on large shopping bags which you provide clients along with your products. Since consumers use these bags twice daily on their long commutes, the scenes may draw attention to both the product and your firm while your customers are still in transit.

Promotion in Informal Markets

Radio is the most effective channel for reaching black market clientele. Radio Metro claims 2.1 million urban African listeners. Radio Nguni & Sotho offers regional coverage in ten languages. The Voice of Soweto can saturate Gauteng, where 45 percent of black adults listen to the radio each day (Morris). Community radio stations operate out of many towns, some universities, and even hospitals, where special programs are beamed to patients. Most former Bantustans (e.g.,Transkei) have stations, while others broadcast to South Africa from Swaziland, Namibia, and Zimbabwe.

Television, however, has the sharpest impact on clientele. Some 30 percent of African consumers watch TV regularly. In Soweto, this rises to 70 percent but drops to 9.8 percent in rural regions. RTV (Rural Television), an independent network covering Ciskei and Transkei (former tribal homelands), KwaZulu-Natal, and Northwest, Northern, and Mpumalanga Provinces, broadcasts directly to rural stores, supplying each outlet with receivers and videos that alternate entertainment and commercials. Once installed on store verandas, a screen draws viewers all day (Morris).

Newspapers have managed only 25 percent penetration in urban African communities. Magazines have a higher readership and more repeat readers, perhaps because they too are dual-use products. Africans rarely throw them away. They not only read them but transform single pages into wall decorations or wrapping. This suggests that advertising should be directed toward print media that feature pictures over text.

To attract repeat readers, advertisements should link one visual image to one slogan, which should vary only slightly over time. Consider Gevalia, a Swedish coffee firm, which has created a theme built on slight variations of the single slogan: "When unexpected visitors arrive." Various ads depict an interplanetary alien, a dragon, and Superman arriving unexpectedly at a tiny Swedish home—whose owner hands each visitor a cup of Gevalia coffee. This type of humor might appeal to informal market clientele. Moreover, since both image and message are simple, retention value would be high.

A less conventional method of promotion is to combine two uniquely South African concepts: "knock-and-drop" and "demo-bakkies." Knock-and-drops are handbills passed out by mobile hawkers who fan out among the neighborhoods. They are least effective when advertising the virtues of a product, most effective when heralding an impending event. Demo-bakkies are flatbed trucks that move slowly and noisily through neighborhoods or open markets at times announced on the hand-bills, similar to an American main-street circus parade in the 1920s.

Ideally, each truck holds a band, since music can lure even the most indifferent passersby. The bakkie parks, a crowd collects, and pitchmen blend story, song, comedy, and commercials to entertain the onlookers. More important, they urge the crowd to chant the product name and slogan, weaving it into a series of the extemporaneous wordplays so beloved in Africa.

Thereafter, discount coupons or product samples are passed out to induce purchase. One company used the demo-bakkie strategy to pass out miniboxes of its product, encouraging recipients to turn in box tops at a specified outlet to receive a free "giant" box in exchange. Once inside the outlet, they were first "offered" (required to watch) a product demonstration, then given the larger box, along with a chance to buy a related product. The goal was to market both the product and the store.

Selling in Informal Markets

Both outlet owners and street hawkers may need to learn how Americans display products to generate client interest. Neither group seems to previously have considered it. Both retail outlets and hawker stalls pile goods rather than display them. Visual promotion may be limited to a single sign that states the obvious ("Shoes for Sale"). Another sign may be placed too high or low for customers to read. Audio promotion may be restricted to shouting or, worse, chanting into a microphone that isn't working well. Color combinations are rarely considered as selling tools, nor is music. Dance is ignored. Lighting is ignored. Scent is ignored.

Begin, therefore, by teaching all of your newly sponsored sales personnel, whether they work in stores or stalls or hawk goods from a blanket, how best to use space to display product images, whether on ceilings, floors, or walls. Next, teach them which colors (and color contrasts) draw attention, particularly the new "electric" colors that are used in the United States but not yet in South Africa. Coca-Cola, for example, now "colors" South African hawker pushcarts, by painting them bright red with the white Coca-Cola logo as well as providing sellers with windup radios to help draw customers (Mallory 1997). However, even colorful displays must be cleaned and maintained to be effective. Thus, a third aspect of training must deal with daily maintenance as a tactic to create sales.

Next, train personnel in the sales value of product demonstrations. These are particularly effective in a marketplace that values relationships, especially where sharing product samples—such as food—both follows African tradition and leads to sales. Stationary demonstrators learn how to interact with clients, thus forming the bonds on which outlet owners depend for repeat sales. Mobile demonstrators visit social centers, churches, schools, and private homes seeking introductions.

Consider the example set by Avon Products, the cosmetics firm, in using product demonstration as a third-world selling tool. The firm operates on three assumptions: that everyone wants to look attractive, that poor women want work, and that more Avon ladies mean more sales. Thus, sixty thousand Avon ladies now travel Brazil's Amazon Basin, seeking customers by kayak, riverboat, and jungle trail (Epstein 1993).

Brazil's Avon ladies begin selling by visiting homes where they are known, then use introductions from these initial contacts to move farther afield. When necessary, they accept goods in lieu of cash as payment for cosmetics, and resell them on the black market to repay Avon and draw commissions. They offer relationship-based credit, since both sellers and buyers anticipate repeat visits and expect the ties they form to last a lifetime. Avon's methods are compatible with both Bantu tradition and black marketing. In South Africa this type of mobile hawking can mean sales.

Finally, introduce your sales staff to post-sales service. Product guarantees may be unknown to either hawkers or outlet owners. As a result, the idea of providing guarantees may meet resistance, for neither group will believe it. To overcome this reluctance, take the concept one step beyond conventional American practice, where buyers with product defects bring or send an item to its maker, then wait weeks for its return. This will fail in South Africa, for few if any clients would send off items in this fashion, believing they would never reappear.

Instead, proclaim that your firm will repair any item at the formal, well-established wholesale site where it is sold. Then, send mobile repair teams to those major outlets on regular schedules. Urge clients to bring problem items for free repairs. While they wait, sellers can offer coffee, samples, demonstrations, and opportunities to buy related products.

Black Market Marketing

Black market marketing reflects the energy and entrepreneurship of those thousands of individuals who are shut out of South Africa's formal economy, who choose to live by their own untiring efforts as an alternative to despair. The sheer intensity of their labor, organization, innovation, and efficiency debunks prevailing Western myths that African workers are ineffective or lazy. Indeed, it has been argued that the official economy need not even function because there is so much energy in the informal one (Schissel). You need only tap into it.

References

Ayers, Ed. 1996. "The Expanding Shadow Economy." *World Watch* (July/August), 11–23.

Birmingham, Steven. 1984. *The Rest of Us: The Rise of America's Eastern European Jews.* New York: Little, Brown, 20.

Cunningham, Anthony, 1991. "The Herbal Medicine Trade: Resource Depletion and Environmental Management for a 'Hidden' Economy." In *South Africa's Informal Economy*, edited by E. Preston-Whyte and C. Rogerson, 196–205. Cape Town: Oxford University Press.

Epstein, Jack. 1993. "Avon Calling in the Amazon." *San Francisco Chronicle* (October).

Evans, Daniel M. Attorney-at law (California) and former Fulbright scholar (Germany). 1999. Personal conversation, November.

Goldberg, Jeffrey, 1997. "Their Africa Problem and Ours." *New York Times Magazine* (2 March), 32–39, 62, 75–77.

Keller, Bill. 1993. "South Africa's Voltage Bandits." *San Francisco Chronicle* (12 September).

Main, Jeremy. 1989. "How to Make Poor Countries Rich." *Fortune* (6 January), 101–106.

Mallory, Maria. 1997. "Carbonating a Continent." *U.S. News and World Report* (5 May).

McIntosh, Alastair. 1991. "Making the Informal Sector Pay: Rural Entrepreneurs in KwaZulu." In *South Africa's Informal Economy*, edited by E. Preston-Whyte and C. Rogerson, 243–53. Cape Town: Oxford University Press.

Morris, Robin. 1992. *Marketing to Black Townships: Practical Guidelines*. Cape Town: Juta & Co., 84–107.

Mosdell, Timothy. 1991. "Power, Patronage and Control: Ambiguities in the Deregulation of Street Trading in Pietermaritzburg." In *South Africa's Informal Economy*, edited by E. Preston-Whyte and C. Rogerson, 326–33. Cape Town: Oxford University Press.

Parker, Joe. 1994. "Entering Informal Economic Sectors in Africa." *Perspectives* 2, no. 3, Corporate Council on Africa, Washington, DC (Summer).

Pender, Kathleen. 1994. "Designer Business Bursts at Seams." *San Francisco Chronicle* (February).

Pilot, Laurence. 1998. Personal correspondence and conversation.

Preston-Whyte, Eleanor. 1991. "Petty Trading at Umgababa: Mere Survival or the Road to Accumulation?" In *South Africa's Informal Economy,* edited by E. Preston-Whyte and C. Rogerson, 262–77. Cape Town: Oxford University Press.

Preston-Whyte, Eleanor, and Sibongile Nene. 1991. "Black Women and the Rural Informal Sector." In *South Africa's Informal Economy,* edited by E. Preston-Whyte and C. Rogerson, 229–41. Cape Town: Oxford University Press.

Rupert, James. 1998. "Trickle-Down Entrepreneurship: Making a Living." *International Herald Tribune* (9 July).

Schissel, Howard. 1989. "Africa's Underground Economy." *Africa Report* (January–February): 43–47.

USA Today. 1999 (26 May).

van Zyl, Maritz. 1992. "The Informal Sector." *The Black Market Report* 7, no. 8 (31 January), 8.

Zulu, Paulus. 1991. "Legitimating the Culture of Survival." In *South Africa's Informal Economy*, edited by E. Preston-Whyte and C. Rogerson, 115–23. Cape Town: Oxford University Press.

10

How to Cope with Crime in South Africa

We shall build…a rainbow nation at peace with itself and the world.

—Nelson Mandela

So, who at this table [a South African business lunch] hasn't been carjacked lately?

—Kathy Chenault

There's a simple equation here: If you get hijacked, your chances of being shot are…between 80 and 90 percent. The young gangsters steal your vehicle and then kill you. It is as simple and stark as that. Gratuitous murder.

—Fergal Keane

The Crime Wave

The final and most important measures you must take while in South Africa are those required to protect your venture against crime. In South Africa, crime is a business problem. Like any other business problem, it can be analyzed and dealt with. I begin discussing the scope of the current crime wave in some detail and then focus on one major cause—a whole generation of so-called "young lions," once at war with South Africa's Whites and now with the society itself. Thereafter, I will describe what firms now in the field are doing to protect their projects, product lines, and personnel.

South Africa is not in chaos. Mandela and Thabo Mbeki have done many things well. A 1996 survey of investment risk ratings ranked African countries from 0 (impossible) to 20 (excellent). It listed Rwanda at 0, Mozambique at 2, Nigeria at 5.32—but South Africa at 16.33 (Lurssen 1996). By 1998 three hundred U.S. firms had invested over 9.5 billion dollars and McDonald's had established 35 hamburger outlets. By 1999 tourism had expanded: 113,000 Americans appeared that year, driving Avis car rentals up 39 percent and nudging Days Inn to launch the first of fifteen hotels in Cape Town. Financially, the budget has been rationalized and the deficit reduced from 10 to 3.5 percent.

Domestically, an African commercial elite has emerged. African-owned firms receive government support. Black unions, co-opted into capitalism, have bought into white industrial consortiums. African capitalists now live in magnificent homes within affluent neighborhoods such as Soweto's "Beverly Hills," employ domestic servants, and drive luxury cars.

These triumphs notwithstanding, South Africa's business community talks mostly about crime. The World Economic Forum places South Africa third (after Colombia and Russia) among nations most affected by organized crime. DRI/McGraw Hill, an economic forecasting service, ranks South Africa as the most precarious investment destination among the ten largest emerging markets (*Natal Mercury* 1997b). South African police list 192 crime syndicates, including 32 with ties to the Russian mafia (diamonds, weapons smuggling), Chinese Triads (trade in endangered species), and Nigerian drug rings (Beresford 1998).

South Africa's crime rate is estimated at twice the global average. Its murder rate (87 slayings per 100,000 people) is about nine times that of the United States, which averages 9 victims per 100,000 people (Lurssen). If the rate of South African murder were applied to the United States, the result would be 140,000 murders per year (*Forbes* 1999). By 1997, South Africa averaged 65 murders, 300 robberies, 42 carjackings, 262 car thefts, and 66 rapes per day (Younghusband 1997). Nearly 34,000 crimes against children were reported in 1998, including 14,225 child rapes (Liebenberg 1999). A rape is reported every twenty minutes (Parker 1997a). Someone is robbed every six minutes. Something is stolen every minute. Some crime occurs every seventeen seconds. Worse, an estimated 55 percent of all crimes are no longer reported (*Finance Week* 1998).

Overseas managers worry most about attacks on their homes. In KwaZulu-Natal, a staggering 48,463 homes and firms were burgled in 1996 (Bissetty 1996). In 1999, the Safety and Security ministry estimated the nation suffered 70,000 residential burglaries and 70,700 in businesses (Loock 1999). In Johannesburg, burglars release gas into the homes they mean to enter, rendering occupants unconscious (Freedberg 1996). Residents in Johannesburg's wealthy suburbs defend themselves by installing steel gates in various sections of their homes to wall themselves off from thieves who do enter. Sometimes, whole buildings are stolen. In April 1999 an entire school was filched, its walls and wiring dismembered and used to build houses in nearby squatter camps (*Economist* 1999a).

The most frequent crime, however, is against cars. In early 1996 ten KwaZulu-Natal motorists were hijacked per day (Jeffrey and Naidoo 1996). By 1996 Soweto's private vehicles were seized at the rate of one every three minutes (Rose 1996). By April 1997 half the ambulances in Soweto had been stolen (*Citizen* 1997). By February 1999 thirty vehicles were already reported stolen from government offices and hospitals in KwaZulu-Natal (Govender 1999). Crime syndicates steal cars to order; supply a photo of the model you prefer and receive it in twenty-four hours (Parker 1997b). Owners respond by installing gear locks, steering locks, door locks, door alarms, and tire boots. These delay thieves but never stop them. Nor do they help against carjacks at urban intersections, where drivers who resist can be shot.

> The directors…of the Afro-Group of Companies…extend their heartfelt sympathies to the family of (name of deceased withheld), a husband and father, as a result of his senseless murder…at the hands of hijackers…. May his loss and that of others like him motivate the authorities to curb the level of criminal violence that pervades our society. (*Natal Mercury* 1996b)

Nor are banks immune; ten are robbed each week. Over R230 million have been stolen since 1994 (*Roca Report* 1997). In the spring of 1997 twenty Johannesburg banks were robbed of over R5 million (Kelly 1997). The sheer frequency of armed robbery so terrorized employees that in May 1997 they staged what must be the first bank tellers strike in history, marching on Parliament to seek protection. As a journalist described it:

> These were not the poor and…hungry. Nor the unemployed. Not even militant feminists or gays…. These were simply bank tellers, and all they were demanding was that the government save them from bank robberies. (Younghusband)

Neither do criminals avoid the political and commercial elite. In one month (August 1996) the president of South Africa's High Court was robbed at home, the minister of justice fled thugs in his home, and a German CEO was murdered in his driveway (*Economist* 1996). Indeed, sixteen of the thirty German CEOs then working in South Africa were attacked in 1996 (*Natal Mercury* 1996a). In 1998 two Swiss tourists were gang-raped near a national park, nineteen American tourists were robbed by a ten-man township gang, and the president of the West Indies Cricket Union was hijacked at gunpoint. In 1999 the head of Korea's Daewoo Motors, South Africa, was shot dead at his gate (*San Francisco Chronicle* 1999), while four foreign businessmen, lured to South Africa, were kidnapped on arrival (Mallet 1999). Is South Africa's primary growth industry actually crime?

The Justice System

South Africa's Police Service (SAPS) is outnumbered, outgunned, underpaid, undertrained, and demoralized. SAPS is understaffed by 22,000 men (Herbst 1996). After 1994 it was radically restructured, as white police at every rank were replaced by former ANC guerrillas as well as semitrained soldiers from the former homelands. Most lacked both law enforcement training and a law enforcement ethic, which resulted in resistance to further training. Some play absentee, with up to 25 percent reporting absent at certain stations. Some are semiliterate and therefore unable to fill out police dockets or charge sheets (Parker 1997b). Some cannot drive—which may account for the R37 million in collision charges levied against SAPS personnel in 1996–97 (*Finance Week* 1997). Some are corrupt; 25 percent of the SAPS officers in greater Johannesburg are now under criminal investigation (Beresford). By 1999 over 30 percent of KwaZulu's 4,500 police detectives had not received detective training (Williams 1999b).

Nor does SAPS command universal respect. Millions of Africans have grown to adulthood with traditions that favor individual or clan action rather than the Western concepts that call for a professional body of law enforcers. In consequence, the very presence of a policeman often invokes hostility. Police cars are ambushed in certain townships after answering fake distress calls. Consequently, officers either ignore *all* distress calls from those areas or enter only alongside armored cars (Younghusband). In 1996 thieves stole property worth R87 million from SAPS itself. In 1997 banks were robbed by gangs wearing police uniforms. By 1999 police cars in both Durban and Johannesburg were periodically grounded, simply due to a shortage of fuel (Williams 1999a).

Police also lack sufficient judicial support from the courts and in prisons. Of every 1,000 crimes committed, only 450 are even reported. Of these, only 230 are resolved, with only 100 prosecuted. Seventy-seven are convicted, but only 36 receive prison sentences, and just eight serve more than two years (*Sunday Times* 1997).

Even among those who do go to prison, few seem to serve out their sentences. The prisons themselves have grown corrupt. In 1996, 1,000 prisoners escaped (Herbst). By mid-1997 350 arrested suspects and incarcerated prisoners were escaping each month from prisons around the country (*Natal Mercury* 1997a). In 1998, 689 prisoners escaped in Johannesburg alone (*Citizen* 1999). As that year ended, an attorney appointed by the minister of correctional services to investigate corruption found an innovative way to prove his case—he smuggled three prisoners out himself. Affidavits signed by prisoners state that an arranged escape costs R10,000 but that lesser sums can buy a night on the town, a wife's conjugal visit, or a prostitute (Vogel 1998). Over 34,000 prisoners have escaped since The Turn in 1994. In 1998 Mandela released 9,000 more to celebrate his eightieth birthday (Boroughs 1999).

Meanwhile, 73 officers were murdered on duty in 1996, while 211 more were killed after hours, and 160 others committed suicide (Braid 1997). By 1999, 1,000 police officers had been killed, perhaps the highest murder rate of law enforcement officers on earth (Boroughs). Many police have simply abandoned SAPS to join private security firms. By 1997 such firms employed 130,000 men, far more than work for the police (*Economist* 1999b). No wonder SAPS is demoralized. How did the crime wave rise so high?

The Tsotsi Generation

No one can pinpoint all the sources of crime. But one source, South Africa's tsotsi generation, impinges so heavily on foreign ventures as to require countermeasures. Tsotsi power springs from historical events unique to South Africa. Remember that in the mid-1970s the African National Congress was still locked in a losing battle with the forces of apartheid. Seeking to make the townships ungovernable, they called an entire generation of African youngsters out of schools across the country. Enthralled by the slogan "Liberation Before Education," tens of thousands responded, abandoning schools to wage street war on Whites for the next twenty years.

They were a generation of self-proclaimed "young lions," armed with slings, stones, garbage lids, and courage. Denouncing their elders as cowards, they went out to do battle. Some went to places like Angola and Algeria for military training and then settled into exile to wage guerrilla war. Most simply stayed in the townships, imposing years of urban terror on the residents as Blacks turned on Blacks, creating chaos in the name of liberation.

In some areas "liberation" took the form of chanting, dancing mobs who set on black police, mayors, councilors, the rich, the respectable, and anyone else they branded as informers. Mobs not only purged specified enemies but also their families, animals, cars, and homes. Justice was dispensed by street committees and people's courts, whose judgments often led to "necklacing" (placing a rubber tire filled with gasoline on the shoulders of anyone they wished to kill).

Do not ignore the real impact of those violent years upon these school-age youngsters. For some, violence was liberating. It gave them purpose.

By the mid-1980s the ANC sought to make the whole country ungovernable. Africans of every age group now joined the youth in a rising wave of noncompliance, refusing to pay rent, bonds, taxes, or for municipal services—whatever was required by the state. In such an atmosphere, lawlessness became synonymous with liberation. As the boldest lawbreakers, the young became the spearhead of the revolution.

By the mid-1990s, perhaps to the amazement of every young lion, they had won their war. The ANC took power. The apartheid laws were repealed, triggering nothing less than mass migration as millions of Blacks flocked from the former home-lands into lives of squatter poverty in the cities. Two million are said to have walked into Durban alone in search of jobs. Only on arrival did these millions realize they had come for opportunities that did not yet exist.

At this point Mandela made his first mistake. He promised that his government would meet their needs, while asking nothing from them in return. Government would provide houses for the homeless, jobs for the jobless, clinics for the ill, electricity against the darkness, water for the thirsty, and education for the unschooled (O'Loughlin 1997). Although the young lions believed him, he failed to draw them into his project by actively soliciting their time, labor, enthusiasm, and, thereby, their loyalty. In short, he gave them nothing to do.

What if Mandela had linked freedom to self-help and hard work? What if he had appeared on TV, on his first day in power, and held up a broom—asking every citizen to seize a broom themselves and join him in sweeping out four hundred years of oppression by cleaning up the townships? Wouldn't virtually every South African have swept and cleaned, working together on that first sweet day of freedom? If Mandela had next held up a hammer, calling on everyone to help their neighbors build more solid homes, with government supplying nothing but materials, would they not have built? And if he had finally held up a police baton and called on citizens to strike down crime, would they not have turned on criminals? In short, if Mandela had put his young lions to work, instead of promising the government would work for them, they might well have responded en masse.

In fact, he asked for nothing but patience. So Africans everywhere now wait and wait and wait until the government provides—school fees, a home, a job. They have waited since The Turn for Saint Mandela to provide—and saints often have this problem: their followers believe what they say.

Sometimes, tired of waiting, they boycott, strike, or riot when the entity they just call "government" fails to provide. Today, university students strike, riot, and withhold school fees, demanding that "government" offer free education. Workers strike, demanding more free time. Renters strike by systematically withholding rent, demanding free housing. TV owners withhold license fees. Drivers ignore traffic fines. The employed evade taxes. Journalists call it a noncompliance syndrome, but many of these people are not rebelling; they are just waiting. They have been offered no other nation-building roles to play.

It is the tsotsi generation, however, that feels most abandoned and betrayed. The very success of their struggle has deprived them of purpose. What can even the most effective street fighter do when the enemy quits and his own side takes power? Lacking schooling, civilian skills, and work-related attitudes, they form the nation's unemployable core. The New South Africa excludes them in two ways: it needs nothing from them and offers them nothing. In sum, they have no mission, no vision, and still nothing to do.

Small wonder many want the liberation struggle to continue and give meaning to their lives. They do not view themselves as criminals but as the same young lions waging the same old war. They define mugging as repayment for oppression, rape as payment for their sacrifice (Collins 1997). A carjacking is considered "repossession." Burglary is "democratic shopping." In short, *a whole generation of young, urban men is still at war with the rest of the nation.* Moreover, they are armed with the powerful and inexpensive weapons that now flood South Africa from foreign lands.

> They smuggle in their AK-47 assault rifles and smuggle out the cars they hijack along the same secret routes they used in their war against apartheid. They are just as ruthless now as they were then; just as prepared to kill, because they have been trained to do nothing else.
> (Younghusband)

South Africans sometimes mislabel this group the "lost" generation. *They are not lost.* Remaining true to their own historical experience, they continue to view lawlessness as liberating. They have been trained by paramilitary experts and honed by years of urban conflict. They practice crime as a viable alternative to lifetime unemployment, poverty, apathy, and despair. Worse, they do it well and in consequence have become the single greatest obstacle to your South African commercial success.

Today's South Africa is like America's West in the 1870s. Police, courts, and prisons do what they can, but the ultimate responsibility must rest with you. To do business in South Africa, you must deal with crime. This means you must either protect yourself or seek the protection of Africans.

Coping with Crime

South Africa's crime wave is not wholly out of control. There has been progress. The nation recently set up its first detective academy, backed by the FBI and Interpol. Parliament has passed new laws tightening conditions for bail and increasing sentences for major offenses. The first anticrime play, *Hola Majita* (*Hello, Gentlemen*), performed by ex-convicts, now plays in townships; its goal is to turn youth against gangs. Most important, surveys of foreign firms suggest that crime has not yet deterred overseas investors. If things are so bad, why do they come?

Since South Africa's crime wave is public knowledge, the investment inflow may be due to the fact that entrepreneurs go where opportunity exists, regardless of risk. It is more likely, however, that companies entering high-crime regions have devised strategies that permit them to cope. Large corporations may hire multinational security services, such as Control Risks Group (London), Defense Systems, Ltd. (London), Executive Outcomes (Johannesburg), Ackerman Security (New York), or Kroll-Ogara Company (New York). These firms, though expensive, will customize security packages to fit your project.

Smaller U.S. companies on limited budgets might prefer to examine four anticrime methods now used by South African firms. These combine elements of camouflage, early warning, evasion, and counterattack. Each combines high technology with common sense to suggest an entire series of effective countermeasures.

Camouflage

This approach assumes you wish to evade the attention of potential criminals by blending into the environment. Begin the moment you arrive. Tone down both your corporate identity and your display of wealth. Omit your company name from landing cards and luggage tags. Do not let high-profile individuals meet you at airports. Bypass airport and commercial limousines. Rent unmarked cars, since logos draw thieves. In airports, use taxis from a major fleet rather than independent drivers. Bypass those with passengers and sit directly behind the driver. Away from the airports shun taxis entirely, thereby avoiding taxi wars. Skip corporate rates at hotels, since they mark you as an executive. Finally, give up attaché cases for standard briefcases and conceal cellular phones, since both signal that you have money (Finney 1996).

Next, camouflage your company presence by blending into the local scene. One option is to segment your operations. Use a variety of names, each likely to draw less attention than that of the firm itself. Or Africanize certain of those operations, joining forces with one or more African firms, using their names, reputations, and staffs to create local identities.

Let us take delivery vans as an example. I noted earlier they might be looted or stoned if rioters believe the vehicles serve white-owned firms. One such firm, Buildware Markets, Ltd., a Johannesburg construction company, has both segmented and Africanized its delivery system by hiring Africans with private trucks and cars to transport materials. This constantly changing, entirely informal fleet, devoid of corporate identification, can move unnoticed and unharmed (Morris 1992).

Early Warning

Camouflage should be supplemented by an early-warning system that employs both in-house security specialists and outside informants. Begin by creating an *in-house watch*, placing at least two of your employees in charge of implementing countermeasures. Ideally, this team should include one American and one African, the latter drawn from the region where you first plan to work.

The American must receive intensive training in the African language and culture of your initial work zone, specifically including proper etiquette. Both men should also complete one of the VIP/Executive protection courses now offered by private security firms in both South Africa and the United States. While providing training in the obvious elements of weaponry, self-defense, and defensive driving, the best of these courses also teach participants to analyze the behavioral patterns used by individuals intent on violence. One overseas executive, for instance, believing himself targeted by potential kidnappers, was able to identify a range of repetitive behavior gang members used to design an ambush:

> For the next six months Jackson became increasingly aware that he was being watched....
> [E]very day a...father, mother and baby sat down for a picnic...immediately opposite his home.
> The "family" changed but the pattern was always the same. (Clutterbuck 1977, 99)

Your African specialist should have a background in local law enforcement. While you may prefer to hire and train your own employee, the fastest way to obtain this expertise is to deal with one of the security firms that now form a South African growth industry, recruiting an experienced man to work for your company at your cost.

The next step is to extend the security system beyond your firm. At this stage, your in-house team must create a *hawker watch*—a web of informants who can be relied on to provide early warning when potential threats appear. This network should consist primarily of the stationary and mobile hawkers with whom your organization deals. Streetwise hawkers depend on local news. Powerless to influence events themselves, they need to learn of incipient unrest in order to evade it. If danger threatens, they will know.

Do not pay them fees for information. These are the people who *must* believe they have a stake in your survival if the early-warning system is to work at all. Rather, provide that steady flow of small gifts and favors (sponsorship, training, etc.) that corresponds to African tradition. As they grow increasingly dependent on your services, they will respond with services in turn, if only to retain you as a benefactor.

Finally, go beyond your hawkers to create a *neighborhood watch*. This will mean incorporating immediate neighbors into your warning system, employing tactics similar to those you use with hawkers. Consider, as one example, the methods used by Conservation Corporation of America (CCA). CCA builds and operates architecturally stunning and extremely expensive wildlife lodges in pristine, rural settings. Its marketing strategy is to keep the lodges isolated, exclusive, and, at U.S.$650 per person per night, quite expensive (McNeil 1997).

To protect its investment, CCA has made a commercial calculation: the more their African neighbors share in the corporation, the greater their dependence on it becomes. The more they depend on it, the more likely they will be to protect it from outsiders—including those who poach animals, steal property, and harm guests. In consequence, the firm incorporates entire African neighborhoods into their warning system, using methods similar to those I suggested earlier for incorporating clans into commercial ventures.

One tactic is simply to employ them all. When building its first game lodge in KwaZulu, for instance, conventional business logic suggested it hire a trained two-hundred-man construction crew from Johannesburg. Instead, it chose a project manager, plumber, carpenter, electrician, and bricklayer, then instructed them to train 250 local laborers in their respective skills (Nevin 1996). The workers were chosen by clan elders rather than CCA staff. Consequently, they came from every home in the community. As the lodge was completed, CCA rehired these same men as cooks, groundskeepers, road crews, housekeepers, charcoal makers, and game scouts, as well as many of the local women to scour the surrounding bush and uproot "alien" (non-African) plants that drive out the indigenous species on which wildlife feeds.

CCA's second tactic has been to provide these same neighbors with commercial opportunity; in other words providing an entire community with a business concept, on-site advice, and a guaranteed market for what they produce. At Bongani Lodge, for instance, CCA introduced its African neighbors to hydroponic vegetable farming in an area too dry to grow grain. The community was taught to farm without soil, raising a crop in nutrient-rich water. CCA provided start-up materials and instruction, while creating new markets for the produce by contacting and influencing upscale supermarkets to act as buyers. In another lodge, African neighbors have been taught to create serviceable stationery from the clean, nonsmelling straw that makes up elephant dung (Nevin). Again, CCA provides a concept, instruction, and markets by selling the stationery in its lodges.

This type of early-warning system is African (not Western) in that it enlists whole communities rather than a few Europeanized elitists. CCA's goal is not charity, but security. If each company headquarters (here, each wildlife lodge) becomes a sustainable generator of wealth for its neighbors, they are likely to protect it. The same applies to U.S. firms in urban areas. Obviously no one, including your neighbors, will stand up for you against armed gangsters, whether rural poachers or urban tsotsis. The ultimate security, however, lies in early warning. One local community member, now a game scout, told me that before the firm came in, the wildlife area where he worked was overrun with nighttime poaching gangs, who cut through fences to catch wildlife in snares. "Now," he said, "when anyone even sees a spotlight in the [game] reserve, they run and run and run until they find us [game scouts], then shout at us that we must get them."

In urban areas, both neighbors and hawkers can provide similar warnings of gang operations and civic unrest. If three informants tell you that carjackers work two specific streets on Friday afternoons or that a trucker's strike will block ten streets next Tuesday noon, you have a basis on which to consider shifting your delivery routes.

Personal Evasion

Personal safety is paramount for you and your staff. Both your company headquarters and personal residence should ideally be located in the upper story of a well-guarded apartment rather than in a freestanding home. Should this prove impossible, each building should have more than one exit and be located on streets that are open to traffic and have no dead ends. If thugs attempt entry, leave first, then take counteraction.

You will be most vulnerable when driving to and from work. Your driveway is dangerous! Clear all concealing vegetation such as vines and bushes away from your gate, driveway, and outer wall. Look both in and under your car each time you approach it, whether at home or in a parking lot. If such lots have security guards, establish a relationship with them. Ply them with small gifts (not cash) and favors, along with explicit instructions to warn you in advance if your car seems threatened, so that you do not confront potential thieves.

When driving, stop far enough behind the car in front of you so you can see the bottom of its tires, thus allowing you to turn evasively if you are threatened while stopped at lights or intersections. If you cannot see the bottoms of the tires, you are too close to turn.

Countermeasures

Camouflage, early warning, and personal evasion must be supplemented by methods to delay, immobilize, and track criminals as well as recover stolen vehicles and goods. Start by arming your home, vehicles, and workplace with devices capable of delaying attackers until you can respond. Delay is different from deterrence. The antitheft devices now used on South African vehicles (tire immobilizer, steering immobilizer, gear immobilizer, etc.) do not deter determined thieves. Nor can the various electronic devices (motion detectors, vibration detectors, handprint detectors, etc.) that protect buildings. Nor do dead bolts, high walls, or iron bars on every window. These measures *can*, however, delay them.

A second step, therefore, is to immobilize intruders, however briefly, until you mobilize defenders. One immobilizing device is the "Radar Watch Dog," a voice recording, using one dog or two, that growls and snarls inside a dwelling at a level of ferocity that increases as intruders approach. In the United States it is meant to deter illegal entry. In South Africa this often fails, since burglars routinely knife dogs that attack them and ignore the noise. However, if set off inside the house, it can be programmed to come from several directions, thus briefly immobilizing looters who are uncertain where to run. In San Francisco, Sharper Image, Inc., offers one- and two-dog versions for around one hundred dollars.

A second immobilizing system, often linked to an infrared motion detector, sprays intruders with a "chili pepper fog," burning the eyes, nostrils, and exposed skin. Composed of a chili pepper extract combined with solvents and aerosol propellants, it sprays up to ten times, each spray disabling victims for half an hour. It can also be placed in vehicles and linked to automatic cellular phone dials that will call police if activated. It has been put into production by a consortium of private security companies, linked to the commercial branch of South Africa's Atomic Energy Commission (Seery 1996).

As intruders are immobilized, the next step is to sound alarms. Some South African executives use bodyguards as living alarms rather than defenders. Rather than cluster these personnel into defensive units, they place them so far apart that the more distant guards escape detection and can radio for help. One Johannesburg firm, for instance, now moves its CEO through high-risk areas in an unmarked car, with a second close behind and a third two blocks further back. The firm's product deliveries follow the same pattern. Trucks deliver from 3:00 to 5:00 A.M., when streets are traffic free and even thugs may be asleep. They move in threes, paced far apart but in view of one another. On reaching an outlet, staff from one truck unload, while the two other crews stand guard at two visible but distant points, to sound additional alarms as needed.

The final step is to recover both vehicles and goods once stolen. To act effectively in this instance, you must once again enlist African allies. Begin by hiring the services of a large, politically connected, well-armed, and highly reliable security firm that has close links to the police. Before signing an agreement, though, attend several segments of its training to verify that trainees are in fact developing a law enforcement ethic in which stopping crime becomes important in their lives. After signing, however, move beyond the contractual clauses to transform the written document into a genuine alliance. Do this by offering such services (e.g., advanced security training in the U.S.) as will render you initially important and eventually indispensable to the firm (Cadman 1996).

Thereafter, link every segment of your electronic warning system to this private firm. *Let it deal with the police.* Have key employees carry pagers or cellular phones, ideally with locking pass codes to protect against piracy. Plant electronic tracking devices in your vehicles without informing staff of their placement. They themselves may be trustworthy, but they will be subject to pressure or even intimidation from kinsmen and comrades who owe you nothing. If they are attacked, train the drivers to press panic buttons, installed beyond the carjackers' range of vision, that allow the device to signal both your security force and company headquarters.

Equip your vehicles with high-tech tracking capability. One option is a remote immobilizing system, such as Intelliguard 900 IQ (BlackJax), sold by Clifford Electronics (Redwood City, California) for three thousand dollars. The driver is equipped with key-chain-sized electronic remote controls. These can arm the system and lock all doors for as many as seven vehicles from one hundred feet away.

If carjacked, you must appear to touch nothing (push no buttons) and simply get out of the car. To resist, even if you are armed, is to risk death by a Kalashnikov assault rifle. Your goal, therefore, is to let the carjacker(s) drive off to the point where they are a safe distance from you. You can then disable the car via phone, dialing a specified code. Then, as the driver either turns or slows down for traffic, the engine automatically shuts off, all lights flash, and a siren blares. The carjacker has little choice but to abandon the car, risking identification from passersby as he leaves. Thereafter, you walk two blocks in the direction the car has gone, deactivate the system with your remote control, get in your car, and drive away (Trink 1998).

Another option is to track stolen vehicles to their final destination by using radio signals. Lojack, Inc. (Dedham, Massachusetts) sells this type of device for approximately six hundred dollars, to be concealed in the vehicle. On learning that it has been stolen, security personnel transmit a coded radio signal; the device responds by sending out a homing beam, allowing the vehicle to be tracked (Marshall 1997).

Another approach is to pinpoint a vehicle location through a satellite-based global positioning system. ATX Research in San Antonio, Texas, charges under two thousand dollars for a system linking twenty-four satellites to a dispatch center and computerized mapping system to track vehicles in response to signals from a panic button. Should carjackers subsequently overwhelm personnel, neutralize the immobilizers, and seize the vehicle, security personnel can locate it to within four meters on a computer screen, then track it as it moves (Chao 1996). Thereafter, they can work with police to intercept and retrieve both vehicle and goods, avoiding the lure of vigilante action by following law enforcement procedures consistent with South African law.

And the Rewards?

In South Africa, providing security for your commercial venture is a normal part of doing business. There can be danger, but South Africa's African market is for neither the conventional nor the timid. It has become a new type of Wild West, an untapped frontier market that should attract commercial pioneers. Other nations have sent out explorers. In KwaZulu alone, trading companies from India, Britain, Taiwan, Singapore, China, Malaysia, and Thailand have now launched business ventures in areas where Americans still fear to tread (Canning 1996). In South Africa, as elsewhere, the rewards are for the bold.

There are also personal rewards for foreigners who find their footing in this market. One is the unremitting optimism of the Africans. You will instantly notice the enthusiasm and exuberance of nearly everyone you meet. There are reasons for this: many feel life has improved; some squatter camps have electricity; one million people now have wells; eight hundred thousand now receive piped water; government-operated welfare programs, inconceivable under apartheid, offer medicine to the ill, pensions for the old, and monthly grants to single mothers (Steele 1997). Every African can now own land. More important, every African now feels free. In the glowing prose of former President Mandela:

> Never, never and never again shall it be that this beautiful land will...experience the oppression of one by another.... [W]e shall build a society in which all South Africans...black and white, will be able to walk tall, assured of their...right to human dignity. (Sparks 1996, 229)

Never again will South Africans endure the unremitting flow of racial insults that so saddened their earlier lives. In consequence, despite the constant turmoil of this nation's early years, these resilient people display nothing of the fatalism one finds in Russia or Ukraine. Instead, their unstinting warmth and kindness will enrich your daily life, and you will find no firmer friends.

There are also personal rewards from working in a land that ranks among the loveliest on earth. So much of South Africa is still relatively unspoiled. Even while conducting business, you will remain aware of the stark, harsh, pristine beauty of the landscapes, so often filled with wildlife, so little changed by humankind. Consider the well-loved words of South Africa's most famous writer:

> There is a lovely road that runs from Ixopo into
> the hills. These hills are grass-covered and rolling
> and they are lovely beyond any singing of it. The
> road climbs seven miles into them…and from
> there, if there is no mist, you look down onto one
> of the fairest valleys of Africa. (Paton 1948, 3)

It is the valley of the Umzimkulu, and there are one thousand other valleys and as many mountains that match its beauty. It is a landscape that can make you shout for joy.

You will find further rewards in the sheer complexity of South African cultures. The nation's history alone will hold you spellbound. The deadly interplay of San and Khoi, Boer and Britain, Zulu and Sotho, White and Black ranks among the most exciting narratives in human history. The country's contemporary music, dance, and drama can be so vibrant and electric as to strike a light inside your soul. There is something about the sheer exuberance of Shakespeare's *Macbeth* played in Zulu, or Gian Carlo Menotti's opera *Amahl and the Night Visitors* sung in Xhosa, that makes whole audiences glow. Finally, South African politics will become enthralling, as you rapidly discover that the headlines in the paper are not merely distant thunder but have direct and often daily impact on your life.

The most singular reward, however, will be your opportunity to become an actor in the new millennium's most thrilling play. The New South Africa has become "The Greatest Show on Earth," in that not one of its almost sixty million performers can guess how their nation's story will end, or even what will happen next. Will it turn to racial violence? Fragment into tribes? Decline to third-world status? Launch an African renaissance? Stagnate? Succeed? No one will say. No one can say.

In the United States, life is often routine. Our workdays are predictable. News headlines rarely have an impact on our private lives. We are confident of our nation's future; America will stay on course. But in South Africa, life is not routine. Workdays are never predictable. News headlines do affect our private lives and often scare us. We have no clue about the nation's future—for the New South Africa does not yet have a course. President Mbeki, in his inaugural address, put it more beautifully than I ever shall. He sees *his* New South Africa as entering

> the dawning of the dawn, when only the tips of
> the horns of the cattle can be seen, etched against
> the morning sky.

Although the darkness lingers for South Africans, we outsiders are twice blessed. We will not only be on site to watch this dawning but can also help to make its history unfold. For when Mandela's rainbow nation finally does emerge from the unceasing storms that symbolize its present turmoil, we will not only have been part of the commerical action, we will have shared the beauty of its birth.

References

Beresford, David. 1998. "S. African Criminals Have Last Laugh." *Manchester Guardian Weekly* (February), 5.

Bissetty, Veven. 1996. "5300 Murdered in KZN." *Natal Mercury* (24 December).

Boroughs, Don. 1999. "Proving that One Man Can Make a Difference." *U.S. News and World Report* (24 May), 36–38.

Braid, Mary. 1997. "A Tide of Crime Swamps the Cops." *The Independent* (London) (29 May), 16.

Cadman, Anthony G. Chairman, Anthony Cadman Associates, South Africa. 1996. Personal conversations.

Canning, David. 1996. "KwaZulu-Natal Plans Investment." *Natal Mercury* (7 March).

Chao, Julie. 1996. "High Tech Tools Foil Car Thieves." *San Francisco Examiner* (17 November), C1, C4.

Chenault, Kathy. 1997. "Cry, the Crime-Ridden Country." *Business Week* (20 October), 30E.

Citizen (Natal). 1999. "Lack of Admin Aids Escapes" (5 January), 1–2.

———. 1997. "Two Gauteng Departments Lashed by Audi-Gen" (22 April).

———. 1996. "SA Crime Hit 7000 Visitors in 1994" (5 March).

Clutterbuck, Richard. 1977. *Guerrillas and Terrorists.* London: Faber and Faber.

Collins, Churton. 1997. "Does South Africa Have the Will?" *Natal Mercury* (12 September).

Economist. 1999a. "South African Education: Heroes into Dunces" (15 May), 46.

———. 1999b. "Behind the Razor Wire" (16 January), 42.

———. 1996. "South Africa: How Wrong Is It Going?" (12 October), 21–23.

Finance Week. 1988. "Crime and Concerned Citizens" (2 October), 15.

Finance Week (South Africa). 1997. "Public Accounts: Blemished Probity" (3–9 April).

Finney, Paul Burnham. 1996. "International Manager: Crime and Punishment on the Road." *International Herald Tribune* (4 April).

Forbes, edited by Joshua Levine. 1999. "Capitalist Odyssey" (5 July), 248–49.

Freedberg, Louis. 1996. "From the Ashes of Apartheid." *San Francisco Chronicle* (28 January), 1, 4.

Govender, Kassavee. 1999. "Hospitals Lose 30 Vehicles in Thefts." *Natal Mercury* (10 February).

Herbst, Jeffrey. 1996. "Will a Crime Wave Spoil South Africa's Political Miracle?" *Los Angeles Times* (11 October).

Jeffrey, Colleen, and Sharda Naidoo. 1996. "Community Acts after Hijack Death." *Natal Witness* (16 September).

Keane, Fergal. 1999. "Gangsters Steal Your Vehicle and Then Kill You. It Is as Simple as That. Gratuitous Murder." *Sunday Telegraph* (South Africa) (17 January).

Kelly, Stuart. 1997. "Armed Robberies Top Tellers' Fear List." *Star* (Johannesburg) (17 April).

Liebenberg, Koos. 1999. "Shock Figures on SA Child Abuse." *Star* (Johannesburg) (15 April).

Loock, Steve. 1999. "18,000 Slain in SA Last Year." *Citizen* (Natal) (19 January).

Lurssen, Neil. 1996. "Super Predators are Mega-Bad." *Washington Letter, Natal Mercury* (14 May).

Mallet, Victor. 1999. "S. Africa Reports Business Abductions." *Financial Times* (South Africa) (25 June).

Mandela, Nelson, President, Republic of South Africa. 1994. Public address to the people of South Africa (10 May).

Marshall, Jonathan. 1997. "Extraordinary Gadget Lowers the Boom on Car Thieves." *San Francisco Chronicle* (14 January), B1, B7.

McNeil, Donald G., Jr. 1997. "Luxury Amid Lions: New Wildlife Safari." *International Herald Tribune* (26 June).

Morris, Robin. 1992. *Marketing to Black Townships: Practical Guidelines.* Cape Town: Juta & Co., 84–107.

Natal Mercury. 1997a. "Stem the Flood of Escapes, Jails Ordered" (18 September).

———. 1997b. "Mbeki Objects to 'Risky' SA Label" (1 August).

———. 1996a. "German Warning to SA Over Crime Levels" (16 August).

————. 1996b. Obituary (name of deceased withheld) (16 July).

Nevin, Thomas. 1996. "People Friendly Tourism." *African Business*, no. 212 (July/August).

O'Loughlin, Ed. 1997. "Mandela's Regime Stumbling." *San Francisco Chronicle* (31 October).

Parker, Aida. 1997a. "The Crime Monster." *Aida Parker Newsletter*, no. 208 (July).

————. 1997b. "The Legacy of Revolution." *Aida Parker Newsletter*, no. 208 (July).

Paton, Alan. 1948. *Cry, the Beloved Country*. New York: Charles Scribner's Sons, 3.

Roca Report. 1997. "Criminal Justice System Close to Collapse?" no. 108 (South Africa) (December), 5.

Rose, Daniel. 1996. "Southern Africa: Try the Beloved." *San Francisco Examiner* (6 June).

San Francisco Chronicle. 1999. "South Korean Auto Executive Killed" (4 February), 11.

Seery, Brendan. 1996. "Hot-As-Chili Security System Is a Gas." *Natal Sunday Tribune* (16 June).

Sparks, Allister. 1996. *Tomorrow Is Another Country*. Chicago: University of Chicago Press, 229.

Steele, Jonathan. 1997. "Post Apartheid Growing Pains." *World Press Review* (14 August), 14.

Sunday Times (South Africa). 1997. "On the Street Where We Live in Fear" (25 August).

Trink, Donald L. Counter-terrorism specialist, Army Reserve. 1998. Personal communications (1 November).

Vogel, Johannes. 1998. "Prisoners Buy Their Way Out…and Hire Prostitutes." *Independent* (South Africa) (21 November).

Williams, Murray. 1999a. "Petrol Runs out at Police Headquarters." *Natal Mercury* (27 January).

————. 1999b. "Many KZN Police Detectives Lack Training." *Natal Mercury* (15 January).

Younghusband, Peter. 1997. "The End of the Dream." *Daily Mail* (London) (24 June).

About the Author

Jeff Fadiman knows Africa. He is a tenured, full professor of global marketing and an African area specialist with thirty-two years of experience. He has taught in South Africa, Kenya, Tanzania, Uganda, England, Germany, Ukraine, and universities across the United States. His forty publications span three academic disciplines: African history, global marketing, and world affairs. Twice an African Fulbright scholar (Kenya, South Africa), he has presented his research to the Stanford Research Institute, California Commonwealth Club, Florida Economics Club, U.S. Navy, and U.S. Department of State.

But Fadiman is more than an academic. He has traveled, lived, and worked with Africans across the continent. In West Africa he joined Songhai and Tuarag traders to canoe the Niger River to Tombouctou (Timbuktu). In East Africa he worked as a bush teacher (U.S. Peace Corps), tribal historian, and Kenyan safari guide. In Southern Africa his research includes ecotourism (Zimbabwe), curriculum development (Swaziland), and urban marketing risk (Zululand). In consequence his orientation is practical. His job is to learn when, how, and why U.S. and African business cultures clash, then offer pragmatic suggestions for resolving their conflicts.

Fadiman's analysis of South Africa's 'Black' market is not for the conservative businessperson. It is meant for risk takers, innovators, and commercial pioneers who wish to cut a new path through South Africa's commercial jungles. This 'Black' market has over forty million African consumers. Beyond it lies another, larger market of four hundred million African consumers, for South Africa is both gateway and launchpad to the continent. Fadiman's goal is nothing less than to teach Westerners to use African methods in these African markets. In one sense, this book is a beginner's guide. In another, it is a survival guide. In every sense it is a marketing guide, providing an intricate and in-depth commercial introduction to South Africa's Africans.